WORKING FOR THE CITY:
You Can't Make this Stuff Up

HOW TO STAND IN TOXIC, TRAUMATIC AND ABUSIVE SITUATIONS

BOSS LADY

Working for the City

Copyright © 2024

All rights reserved.

Published by Red Penguin Books

Bellerose Village, New York

ISBN

Print 978-1-63777-627-8

Digital 978-1-63777-626-1

No part of this book may be reproduced in any form or by any electronic or mechanical means, including information storage and retrieval systems, without written permission from the author, except for the use of brief quotations in a book review.

Judge me by my cover and you'll miss my story

— (REAL HOUSEWIVES OF SYDNEY)

CONTENTS

The Purpose/Overview	vii
1. Self-Reflection	1
2. A Hot Mess	17
3. A Fresh Start?	54
4. The Person Who Hires You	76
5. The Heart is Deceitful	108
6. Side Bar	124
7. Keep it Going and Keep it Moving	126
8. Power Points	131
9. I Now Realize	134
10. Keys	138
11. The Conclusion	151

THE PURPOSE/OVERVIEW

This memoir is written to convey a message to readers, retirees, government workers, corporate workers and housewives who are married to someone who abuses their authority. It's about people who destroy others to make themselves feel or look better. A message that will hopefully make you realize that "You are not alone."

Additionally, where I didn't know that I was me, I want to offer awareness. Awareness of self, awareness of people, awareness of trauma, fear, hopelessness and helplessness. I will share stories that could unnerve you and have unnerved me and I have come to learn that no one wants to talk about these issues, no one wants to believe in the existence of these issues and no one wants to acknowledge these issues-including those in authority.

You will also notice that while I'm sharing my story, I have included some research opinions to emphasize a point.

Self awareness was amply captured by Mark Goulston and Philip Goldberg, authors of "Get Out of Your Own Way: Overcoming Self-Defeating Behavior," and it speaks to how to stop being your own worst enemy and become your own best friend," which is what I had to learn to do through these painful experiences. Also, I will say to you what author Adam Marburger said, *"You're the F*cking Problem, You are the problem. You have always been the problem. Does that sting a little? It's tough hearing the bold truth at times. The reality is that the truth hurts. Being self- aware is one of the best qualities one can possess. If you are unwilling to be self-aware or unable to do so, it will keep you from growing to the next level."*

However, this is not a normal memoir, it's a book of thoughts and adventure that I've encountered over the years. As I have shared my thoughts about my life, you too will have an opportunity to share your thoughts with thought provoking questions that we don't tend to ask ourselves or at least I didn't until I decided to write my thoughts. Join me in writing down your thoughts after each chapter and take a look at who you are as I had to do. Each chapter was carefully crafted with you in mind. Use this memoir to help you circumvent some unnecessary hardships and learn from my mistakes.

I hope you will capture and understand the overflow of my memoir as its multi-layered and self-reflection is at the center of it all. As an added delight I have chosen to weave in and highlight some spiritual lessons and moral truths.

The other reason for this memoir is to share my personal experiences, opinions and appraisals during and after my employment with government agencies. However, this is not limited to just the community of government employees but it's for everyone who has worked and has encountered the same types of behaviors and experiences. I hope you will find some solace that these experiences are factual and happened often enough for me to memorialize. Whatever you are going through is neither a figment of your imagination and may not necessarily be **your fault**. Although my experiences have had some challenges, there were some rewards as well. The use of word pictures (i.e. Smirky smiley face) will hopefully add humor and imagination. You will find a mixture of conversational sections, general advisory sections and reflective sections.

Some readers may think and say, "Well this happens everywhere and everyday so why are you writing about it"? Well the answer to that question is, I wanted to write about my experiences for a few reasons:

- Primarily, I believe that these experiences should not be bottled up inside me. I find it important to get it out of my mind, my will and my emotions.
- Secondly, I firmly believe that those who come after me will read this book and realize that they did not know themselves. It is important for people to realize the "truth"—even about themselves. *Pause and calmly think about that.*
- Thirdly, I no longer wanted to be mentally stuck in my situation.
- Lastly, I wanted to reconfigure my mental and spiritual life.

At some point I have chosen to confront myself and to work on becoming a well-balanced person and I hope that you will see that as you read. I realize that pointing one finger at others while three fingers are pointing back at you (me) is actually unhealthy.

My parents separated when I was about six or seven years old and I distinctly recall one of my favorite events growing up was on the weekends. My mother would either have company and they played cards which were either "big wes" although I believe the proper name is "bid whist" or spades; or she and her friends would go out to party. Either way, I enjoyed sneaking a sip of my mother's "cold duck," which I believe was a malt liquor, while she was getting ready and the music was playing loudly. *Dancing emoji*

Back in the day, as they say, business schools were the choice of education in most urban neighborhoods-so I attended a business school and earned a certificate in Word Processing. During that time, Word Processing was the "go to" in order to make a decent salary without a college degree. Around the age of 21, I moved out of the projects where I lived with my mother, brother and sister. After losing my job in corporate America I applied for welfare and was a welfare recipient for about two-three months. In hindsight I did not apply for unemployment and I don't know why. Perhaps because my mother worked for about 30 years in the welfare department with the government and applying for welfare was a familiar and unconscious way to go. I'm purposely using the word *welfare* because that's what it was called at that time. After about a couple of months I started applying for government jobs-which took some time but eventually came through. So I moved on from there.

I moved on from there and am now a survivor, a mother of an adult child, a college graduate with a Master's degree, a retired government employee, a homeowner, a paralegal, a substitute teacher, an entrepreneur and an author.

Moving on is a decision, as it will allow you to be present for your future. So, enjoy the book, absorb the truths, laugh at the foolery, recognize your pain, sit in it, feel it, and move on.Move on from poverty, move on from fear, move on from abuse, move on from sickness, move on from loneliness, move on from jealousy, move on from pride– just move on.

Hopefully, my experiences and the information provided will help you to put a "handle" on things much better and much sooner **than I had.**

I want my memoir to impact your thinking to keep you moving forward and help you to never give up on life. To quote Pastor Charles Stanley, "This (my) book is born out of my hurts."

"One day you will tell your story of how you overcame what you went through, and it will be someone else's survival guide" Brene Brown.

While watching the *Becoming* Documentary on Former First Lady Michelle Obama, she made the following statements that helped me to put a better handle on why I wanted to share my story (italics mine)

> *making the decision to* become unplugged and
> *to be willing* to share a set of experiences
> Creating my next track
> Wanted to create bridges
> Dare to be vulnerable

While working at a retail store fulfilling people's orders, I had a great opportunity to self-reflect. I realized that I was so wrong in so many ways while employed with the government. I began to realize that perhaps my adversaries were right about me, and I better understood why they hated me and why they were laughing at me. I thought, wrongfully, that I was all of that and a bag of chips. How did I go from being middle management making a six-figure salary to fulfilling online shopping orders. I would sometimes ask myself, *what happened to me?* Then I would immediately realize that this was good for me. I needed this kind of wake up call. I needed to see myself through a different set of lenses because I was the common denominator. *This is good for me,* was the constant reminder that came to the forefront of my thinking and perspective. I was becoming a better person. If I was to return to the workforce, I would go back to being a better person.

I wanted to be careful not to focus so much on other people or my colleagues because I want to highlight some lessons learned and realized, after-the-fact, to have someone to learn from my past failures and/or mistakes.

The roar that I had was very much misguided and a bit crazed. However, life has taught me that "roars" could be helpful as well as damaging. Watch how and why you "roar."

But as a reminder, this memoir is written post-retirement. I had time to really self-reflect. I see things very differently now. I have become more aware of any drama that I may be generating within a situation. I have now purposed that there will be "no more drama" in my life by the special Grace of the Almighty God.

I've had time to listen to the inner tears and cries, not knowing why. But I'm now aware of what is going on inside me and beginning to really tune into myself. I now ask myself; how can I diffuse a situation rather than feeding into it realizing that it's not worth all the potential drama. I see people clearer, their behavior clearer and potential motives too. I do this keeping in mind that I must first remove the plank out of my own eye before I can remove the speck of dust from my brother's eye. (Matthew 7:4-5)

Self-confrontation or self-reflection is not easy but very necessary to move life forward.

At the end of each chapter, I have included lessons that I have learned and prayers that I wish I had prayed during those times. Mostly, I became aware of how unaware I was [of myself]. Little self-awareness and self-reflection.

Consider the lessons in the next chapter.

CHAPTER 1
SELF-REFLECTION

Did you ever think of your own thoughts, or question yourself about your mental processes?

Do you occasionally take time in a moment of doubt or uncertainty to clarify your values?

If your answer is "yes," then you are no stranger to self-reflection and introspection. Self-reflection is an important psychological exercise that can help you grow, develop your mind, and derive benefit from your past mistakes.

Taking the chance to reflect is something of a forgotten art. Unfortunately, most of us are living uncharted lives. So, what is self-reflection exactly? And what are the easy ways to bring it into practice?

SELF-REFLECTION: AN ANALYSIS

To put it simply, self-reflection means to take the time to think about, meditate, analyze, and give your habits, emotions, beliefs, motives, and expectations significant consideration. It's the method of immersing your feelings, emotions, and motives profoundly and deciding the perfect, "Why?" behind them.

Self-reflection helps you to examine both a macro and a micro aspect of your life. At a global stage you can determine your life's overall tragedies. You can see where you are going, decide whether you are comfortable with the route and make changes if appropriate.

Reflection is a deeper mode of learning that helps one to maintain any part of every **event that happened in life**, whether it's personal or professional—why this happened, what the effect was, whether it could happen again—as compared to merely recalling it occurred. It's about digging into every part of the world, clarifying our thoughts, and honing in on what's most important to us.

Practicing self-reflection depends upon both patience and willfulness. It takes a break from the stress of life and just takes the time to think about your life and learn about it, which is not an easy thing for many people. Yet it is an extremely rewarding task.

IMPORTANCE OF SELF-REFLECTION

We simply go about life without thinking, without self-reflection, jumping from one thing to the next without taking the time to determine what is really going on. We cease to pause for reflection. Analysis. We fail to decide what works, and what does not. The tragic outcome is we get trapped sometimes in a vicious cycle.

For example, a lack of personal reflection, may lead us to remain in a job we don't like or a relationship that will not go well.

A lack of contemplation effectively allows one to keep going, trying to compromise even if things aren't working out. We just seem to learn how to keep our heads above water. We have eventually ended up repeating the same things constantly, **even though those things didn't produce the outcome we had wished for.**

THE BENEFITS OF SELF-REFLECTION

Well, finding time for **self-reflection can be** tough. Taking the time to step back and try to grasp what matters, can be difficult. Even then, there are some significant benefits of self-reflection, and we can all make time for that.

It Allows You to Gain Perspective

Emotions might affect your judgment and you might lose sight of what really matters. Some things appear larger and worse than they really are.

Self-reflection enables you to take a step backwards and gain insight into what matters and what can be ignored. It allows you to process and understand experiences.

It Helps You Respond More Effectively

For most of the time, we're only leading to the situations we go through. That can lead us to say and to do things that we reconsider. When we are in a responsive mood, we don't take the time to consider our actions and expressions. Personal reflection allows you to consider the consequences of your words and actions. It also enables you to consider the best, most effective, most helpful way to act in a given situation.

It Promotes Learning and Understanding

We don't learn or develop a better understanding of reality as we go through it, without pausing to stop and reflect. We only switch from one aspect to another, without taking breaks to think about what important lessons we might learn.

On the other hand, self-reflection helps one to analyze and evaluate what you've learned. It helps one to think profoundly and learn about the importance of our situations, feelings, and motives. It encourages one to live a balanced, equitable and safe life.

WHY REFLECTION IN THE WORKPLACE?

Employees usually learn and develop new skills in the workplace through learning and development exercises such as hands-on training or games in cultured cells—with no time for reflection. Lacking the chance to think, projects are much less successful at bringing in meaningful reform, with workers frequently preferring the status quo. Here's why: after a person has gained a certain amount of experience with a job, the gain of further experience is in effect less than the gain extracted from devoting time to focusing on the experiences they have already had.

Put it simply, knowledge has a point of diminishing returns. We really can't understand more by doing more. We all need to consider what we have done to improve and develop.

Results showed that self-reflective workers, especially those who observe and share their experiences with others, performed substantially more than those who simply studied. For consumer loyalty among all groups, those who self-reflected were also far more likely to be in the top-rated group. Employees can further incorporate learning and view jobs from an enhanced state of consciousness and motivation when incorporating meditation.

MAKE REFLECTIVE THINKING A HABIT

In an environment that supports you and away from your desk and computer, and when you are in a positive state of mind, it is important to allocate at least 10-15 minutes for reflection a few times a week. And you're in the morning or evening at its best? When is your mind handled, observe out?

To create the best situations for recognizing your intentions and trying to help you hear and understand your thoughts and feelings, turn off all background noise and devices.

Trying to capture reflections is also helpful even though one's insights and ideas can be fleeting.

The Reflection Toolkit

Reflection requires a few skills which can easily be developed.

- **Self-awareness–** an ability to pause, to pay attention to thoughts and feelings and to self-question non-judgmentally. This will help you to become aware of your habitual ways of thinking and behaving in any given situation.
- **Description–** it is important to be able to describe/recall situations neutrally. These questions can help. What did I see and feel happening? What background factors played a role? What were the things under my control? How would other people involved describe me and the situation?
- **Critical analysis–** the ability to challenge your assumptions by asking yourself: Is what I am thinking about myself, others, or the situation true? Where do I need to focus next?

- **Review**– an ability to pause and to ask:'What would I do differently next time and why? How exactly will I do it and how will that give me the outcome I want?'
- **New learning and next steps**– an ability to learn about yourself from experiences (your potential and areas for improvement) rather than seeing yourself or others as a failure.

Ask yourself: What have I learned about myself? How can I use my potential best? Where is my biggest area for improvement?

I regularly use these tools to reflect. To gain clarity about what worked and what didn't work so well, to gain insights into limiting beliefs and assumptions, key learnings and where to focus next.

Apply these tools for reflection to anything, big or small—they will add depth to how you live your life, rendering it more satisfying and meaningful as a result.

ALTERNATIVE REFLECTION MODELS

Here are four potential ways to reflect, depending on your preference.

Self-talk

Having a conversation with yourself in the form of questions and answers.

Reflective Writing

When we write things down, we support the process of reflection because when we write thoughts down, we "objectify" them. Our thoughts are now on the page, ready and waiting to be referred to. When we sit down to think, our thoughts can sometimes be elusive.

Reflective Walking

Reflecting while walking is powerful. I have my best ideas when I'm out and about—hence my 'coaching while walking' approach. When we walk our brain waves slow down, clearing the mind for fresh thinking and ideas. Many well-known thinkers recommend reflecting while walking as an aid for thinking: Nietzsche said: 'All truly great thoughts are conceived by walking.'

Reflecting With Others

This can be done as a pair or in a group. Firstly, decide on a topic you want to reflect on e.g. an upcoming project, reviewing a report, an important decision etc. Assign someone as a listener (the listener will also be the timekeeper). The listener's role is to listen attentively for 10 minutes to the speaker's reflections on the given topic. If there are silences, that's fine too. The roles then swap.

After everyone has had a chance to reflect aloud, go into another round of reflecting about what you've heard. Five minutes each is often enough. You can continue until the process comes naturally to an end. Note taking is useful to ideas and new insights.

Reflection can be a very empowering process. It can help you to make sense of your day; to come to decisions, to set a course of action; to step away from your habitual way of doing and thinking and discover new freedoms and opportunities.

SELF-REFLECTIVE QUESTIONS TO ASK YOURSELF

There are nearly endless questions, prompts, and ideas you can use to take a self-reflection break. Some of these can be asked, answered, and addressed every day, while others may best be saved for occasional self-reflection.

Answering them can take you from feeling like you don't understand yourself to knowing yourself like the back of your hand.

These 10 questions are great ways to jumpstart self-reflection.

- Am I using my time wisely?

- Am I taking anything for granted?

- Am I employing a healthy perspective?

- Am I living true to myself?

- Am I waking up in the morning ready to take on the day?

- Am I thinking negative thoughts before I fall asleep?

- Am I putting enough effort into my relationships?

- Am I taking care of myself physically?

- Am I letting matters that are out of my control stress me out?

- Am I achieving the goals that I've set for myself?

The following 30 questions are questions you can ask yourself every day to get to know yourself better.

- Who am I, really?

- What worries me most about the future?

- If this were the last day of my life, would I have the same plans for today?

- What am I really scared of?

- Am I holding on to something I need to let go of?

- If not now, then when?

- What matters most in my life?

- What am I doing about the things that matter most in my life?

- Why do I matter?

- Have I done anything lately that's worth remembering?

- Have I made someone smile today?

- What have I given up on?

- When did I last push the boundaries of my comfort zone?

- If I had to instill one piece of advice in a newborn baby, what advice would I give?

- What small **act of kindness** was I once shown that I will never forget?

- How will I live, knowing I will die?

- What do I need to change about myself?

- Is it more important to love or be loved?

- How many of my friends would I trust with my life?

- Who has had the greatest impact on my life?

- Would I break the law to save a loved one?

- Would I steal to feed a starving child?

- What do I want most in life?

- What is life asking of me?

- Which is worse: failing or never trying?

- If I try to fail and succeed, what have I done?

- What's the one thing I'd like others to remember about me at the end of my life?

- Does it really matter what others think about me?

- To what degree have I controlled the course of my life?

- When all is said and done, what will I have said more than I've done?

Finally, the following prompts and questions are great ways to put your journal to use:

- My favorite way to spend the day is . . .

- If I could talk to my teenage self, the one thing I would say is . . .

- The two moments I'll never forget in my life are . . . (Describe them in great detail, and what makes them so unforgettable.)

- Make a list of 30 things that make you smile.

- "Write about a moment experienced through your body. Making love, making breakfast, going to a party, having a fight, an experience you've had or you imagine for your character. Leave out thought and emotion, and let all information be conveyed through the body and senses."

- The words I'd like to live by are . . .

- I couldn't imagine living without . . .

- When I'm in pain—physical or emotional—the kindest thing I can do for myself is . .

- Make a list of the people in your life who genuinely support you, and whom you can genuinely trust. Then, make time to hang out with them.

- What does unconditional love look like for you?

- What things would you do if you loved yourself unconditionally? How can you act on these things, even if you're not yet able to love yourself unconditionally?

- I really wish others knew this about me . . .

- Name what is enough for you.

- If my body could talk, it would say . . .

- Name a compassionate way you've supported a friend recently. Then, write down how you can do the same for yourself.

- What do you love about life?

- What always brings tears to your eyes? (As Paulo Coelho said, "Tears are words that need to be written.")

- Write about a time when your work felt real, necessary, and satisfying to you, whether the work was paid or unpaid, professional or domestic, physical or mental.

- Write about your first love—whether it's a person, place, or thing.

- Using 10 words, describe yourself.

- What's surprised you the most about your life or life in general?

- What can you learn from your biggest mistakes?

- I feel most energized when . . .

- Write a list of questions to which you urgently need answers.

- Make a list of everything that inspires you—whether books, websites, quotes, people, paintings, stores, or stars in the sky.

- What's one topic you need to learn more about to help you live a more fulfilling life? (Then, follow through and learn more about that topic.)

- I feel happiest in my skin when . . .

- Make a list of everything you'd like to say no to.

- Make a list of everything you'd like to say yes to.

- Write the words you need to hear.

Write down your thoughts and questions about this chapter. Write it down and make it plain (Habakkuk 2:2-3)

_____

_____

_____

_____

_____

_____

_____

_____

_____

_____

_____

The following chapters are events that occurred pre-retirement which brought the realization of the need to self-reflect. Do you see yourself in these events?

_____
_____
_____
_____
_____
_____
_____
_____
_____
_____
_____

CHAPTER 2
A HOT MESS

"How could you hire me and then want me to be stupid?" Bishop TD Jakes

WHAT HAPPENED?

One rainy morning, The Lord led me to go to fill out a job application on Court Street where I did not have an interview, nor a meeting and I was simply going to fill out an employment application. During those days, you were allowed to go to Court Street to fill out a job application. So, I wore wrinkled jeans and a shirt, an unflattering jacket, a cap, and no make-up. I looked like a hot mess. So, I rushed to the Customer Service Counter and informed one of the worker's that I wanted to apply for a job. I was then given an application form, took a seat, completed the form, and submitted it at the Customer Service Counter along with my resume. I was instructed to go back to my seat and wait while the worker looked at my resume. A few minutes later I was called to a window and was instructed to go to another floor within the same building. I moved towards the elevator to go to the other floor wondering about how I looked, because I was not ready for an interview. When I reached my destination, I was guided towards a room. By entering the room I saw several people there already waiting to be called for an interview. I sat down on a chair and minutes later my name was called and I was then directed to go into a back room to be interviewed. I was asked a few questions about my work experience after which I went back to have a seat. Minutes later I was given a piece of paper and was told to go across the street to another building on Livingston Street.

I went there with that piece of paper in my hand and after being interviewed for the second time, I was interviewed for the third time with the Office Manager. I was hired for a temporary position as an Executive Assistant to the General Counsel under the condition that I start that same day. Try telling me that wasn't God. Oh and by-the-way, please keep in mind what I looked like that day.

This was my first government job and I'm telling you it was an experience.

After working in this temporary position for a couple of months, I was asked to stay on as a permanent employee to handle all things purchasing, and I accepted the offer. There my duty was to report to a Jewish woman who was there for many years. I was informed by the *"veteran"* workers that my supervisor had an emotionally unstable child, lived with her sickly mother, and had another child who was out of control. Therefore, according to the veterans, she could not give her full attention to work and was out of the office—a lot. So, when I was asked to stay on as a permanent employee, I didn't refuse because to me it was a no brainer. I started working the same day with my supervisor who was the Office Manager. She trained me in all things purchasing-because she hated it. She just wanted to do budget. Okay fine, not a problem. I became well-versed in purchasing as that was my sole focus, as it was my first time realizing how purchasing worked in the world around me and in the world period.

My supervisor came to the office off and on to check on things, she realized that I was absorbing my role as I thought she wanted and expected me to do. I became more noticeable day-by-day with the staff and the attorneys as they required specific supplies for their cases and I had to deal with them every day. Oh by-the-way, I worked in an office where there were well over 30 attorneys. The attorneys were always in need of the legal-size expanding folders-it was an ongoing issue. People came to me to submit their purchasing needs and I would prepare all the necessary documents for either a bid, a small purchase, or a micro purchase. During that time, emails were not utilized as much then as it is now, use of technology was not so common. So, I met with my supervisor regularly to give her reports and would update her on any work issues or potential projects.

During my first year on the job, I applied for an exam as a secretary because I had just missed the exam for Purchasing Agent. The "veteran" workers urged me early on to become a permanent city employee so that should layoffs occur, I would not be impacted. So as a single parent, I jumped to the opportunity because I had responsibilities. I was given the name of the person in Human Resources to contact because the deadline to apply for taking the exam had just passed. However, when I went to the Human Resources Department and met with the director, I told her that I was interested in taking the Secretary's exam because I was new to government employment and missed the deadline. The Director, at that very moment, made a call on my behalf and was given the approval for me to immediately submit my application to take the exam. The filing fee was waived and I was approved to take the secretary exam which was a few months away. Again, it was Divine Intervention and favor for me, I know. God, won't He do it?!

Some of my colleagues and human resource personnel directed me to purchase the testing manual for the Secretary's exam, to provide some insight into the actual exam. I studied hard for the exam and succeeded.

Yahoo! I aced the exam with a perfect score of 100 and the next step was to wait for the list to be generated, to be assigned a "list number" and to be "picked-up" off the list.

While waiting for the Secretary's exam list to be generated, I had time to do something for my career and after thinking about it I decided to register for school. I wanted to finally complete my bachelor's degree. I attended the College of New Resources with a concentration in Psychology. I recall my supervisor saying to me that she had never seen anyone move up as fast as I did and from that day on our relationship began to change because I became a threat to her-unbeknownst to me at that time.

During my school days, I met a lot of great people including teachers as they too were government employees. During our class introduction, the professor of Introduction to Public Administration, announced that he never gives out "A's" because he does not believe in them." Well, I didn't know about the other students but that was the wrong thing to say to me. We had to write a paper on a topic of our choosing. My paper was on "Abuse of Power." In my paper, I first defined the words *"abuse"* and *"power"* (respectively). By the time my professor finished reading my paper I received an A++ with the following words, "I have never read such an original paper like this."

The following are excerpts from my paper.

> "According to Webster's Dictionary, abuse means to mistreat, to insult, revile and power means authority, influence. Therefore, it can be said that abuse of power is mistreated authority/influence, or we can simply say misuse of authority/power. I further wrote that, "Within the workplace abuse of power is quite

common and it happens daily in every office, business, and company. Misused authority happens when people are given absolute authority, and their behavior and decisions go unchecked and unchallenged. The abuse is disguised in many ways and often gives the appearance that it's done 'in the line of duty.'"

If an individual is granted authority, he immediately gets the power and can use it in any way. Abuse of power happens when a person in command misuses the power imposed upon him to perform an illegal act for personal gain or other purposes. Workplace's abuse of power is often called "malfeasance." Any misuse of power, such as sexual harassment, neglect, physical assault, etc. are considered as abuse of power. No matter what community you are in or organization you serve, you will often come across people who use their authority to take advantage of their rank and abuse people who work for them.

There was much more about abuse of power in my paper but coming back to the story of my job, some of my responsibilities were to purchase supplies, equipment (i.e., computers, printers, etc.) and furniture; I had to negotiate prices with contracted vendors; to resolve any service discrepancies and to make sure vendors were paid in a timely manner. Abuse of power is something I experienced frequently on my job and despite what I did, my supervisor always found something wrong and made an issue out of it.

Her main pattern of behavior was to play the victim, which meant that if she didn't get her way she would manipulate and manufacture a story to senior management stating that I was either doing something wrong or not doing something which they would believe thus, whatever it was that she wanted, she was able to get it. For example, she wanted me to provide her with a report on checks to vendors, the amount and purpose of the payment. She knew and I knew that this information and more was generated by the city specifically down to our division as there were certain budget codes that we used to obtain this information. However, those in authority were unaware of this component and although I tried to tell senior management that this information was automatically generated by the city which would be a duplication of duties if I were to provide it. The manner in which my supervisor manufactured the need for me to prepare this report unnerved them, thus I was required to provide this report. She had them believe that without this information/report she had no idea what was being purchased and the monies spent. So I generated this report for a short period of time and slowly I would "forget" to do the report and after a while my supervisor no longer wanted me to generate this report as she privately confessed to me that she can always look on the city's link to obtain the report. You see I knew that she just wanted her way and after she got her way, after a while it was no longer an issue for her, although senior management was under the impression that I was still generating this report for my supervisor.

She would also go through my files and remove them without my knowledge or consent mostly whenever I was out of the office. When I realized that the files were missing, I would ask her about the files, and she always became defensive and tried to prove me wrong. To defend herself she would go to the First Deputy, who was her supervisor, to tell her that I was accusing her of taking my files. Then the First Deputy, who was an elitist, easily agreed with my supervisor and told me that I didn't have the right to question my supervisor and I shouldn't do that.

So, I remained *verbally* silent and never said a word in return. Whenever a vendor called to say that a payment hadn't yet been made because copies of their invoices were missing I was unable to dispute it and it would be totally insane. So, to get rid of this shameful excuse of not having the invoices, with the vendors, I requested another copy of the invoice, prepared all the paperwork again for the payment to be made and as soon as a check was sent to the vendor a copy of the original payment suddenly appeared in my file, thus it showed that a double payment was made to the same vendor. After which I had to confront my supervisor and her supervisor that this tactic is unacceptable and the result of her (my supervisor) taking my files without any notification is double payments to the vendor and because my name was on these documents, I was not negotiating on this and I took it to our general counsel and he directed my supervisor to notify me if and whenever she removed my files.

After this incident, I knew that my supervisor was trying to set me up. I did not understand the matter, because there was no reason why she should be pulling my files anyway, because she was handling the budget, and I was handling purchasing. But my supervisor had convinced the First Deputy [who was a white woman] that she must have access to my files. They were not agreeing with me, but my point was valid, that if my supervisor needed access to my files, why did she always wait until I was out of the office-even if it was for one day and would not leave a note informing me that files have been removed. I had gone through many of these types of issues, which was very upsetting for me. But believe me, I had my ways of getting her back and a couple of those ways were confronting her with the truth that she was trying to set me up and the other way was to just tell her off about whatever came to my mind and it drove her crazy. (*Smirky smiley face*)

I was asked to move on the opposite side of the floor and 6 months later I had to move back on the other side of the floor. There was no real reason that was given for this abrupt decision, but the surface excuse was that since I moved over to the other side of the floor the communication between my supervisor and I had gotten worse. Although we did not communicate when we were on the same side of the floor. There was not any acceptable reason for that movement. All I can say is that it did not go well for her or our relationship. That's all I'm going to say.

The First Deputy was new to the department and believed everything my supervisor said, to her own detriment, so her influence was being misused and my manager gloated when she had her way.

Within a particular unit, two of the attorneys (one supervisor and staff attorney) who worked together for over 10 years and had a very strained relationship, then the staff attorney was promoted over his supervisor, an older gentleman, and he took full advantage of it by assigning more contracts to his former supervisor than the other attorneys and would unnecessarily harass him-just because he could. Needless-to-say, the former Deputy was devastated and ashamed and to add insult to injury he was transferred out of that office to another location. Most of us were heartbroken for him and felt helpless. This newly appointed Deputy did this because he knew that the First Deputy was not going to say anything, so he did whatever he wanted to his former supervisor. Why? Because he could. Also, this newly promoted attorney was a real *yahoo*. A case in point that comes to mind is while his mother was on her deathbed, he had her sign over a car to him that he wanted and did not want his siblings to have. On his mother's death bed. (Addendum mine).

For the purpose of my school assignments, I was very descriptive about my supervisor's every move and interaction with me and others. Whenever there was trouble in the office, she loved it and would often glee whenever someone was in trouble. My school papers were often based on my true everyday experiences and how my supervisor (and others like her) got away with so much abuse and corruption, my classmates loved it because they were able to identify with my experiences.

Although they laughed as I shared my stories via reading out loud assignments, many of my classmates would come to me privately and say that they knew firsthand what I was talking about. That was no laughing matter. *Pause and calmly think about that.*

In my Criminal Justice System class, I did a report on "Men: Victims of Domestic Abuse." In this report I was able to cite, statistically, that men were far more victims of abuse than women but is grossly underreported. My research showed that when men attempted to make reports about being physically and/or emotionally abused by their loved ones, they were shunned by the legal system. This paper so resonated with my professor that she asked me if she could have a copy of my paper to give to a close male friend (who was an attorney) because he was experiencing that very issue. I always tried to write about matters of the heart because that is what I was experiencing at the time, abuse, abuse of authority (power)-but mine was in the workplace or was it.

I was now a permanent government employee. Although I was doing the work of a purchasing agent, my office title was Secretary. With government, you could have an office title and/or a civil service title which differed for each other.

I think it's important for me to share that my predecessor was fired and humiliated because she used a budget code (was probably instructed to do so) in procuring a file cabinet. My understanding of the story is that there were two budget codes for this item. However, one was more general than the other. Not that either budget code was really wrong, but they were subjective. It was really left to one's discretion. Well, allegedly she used the "wrong" code-although it was approved by the Office Manager (my future supervisor), she was humiliated by news reports of misuse of budget codes-the newspapers were called and did a report on the issue, and she lost her job. However, the Office

Manager went undetected, untouched and unphased about the matter. Apparently, my predecessor was crying hysterically in the office and the Office Manager remained unaffected by this woman's humiliation and distress. You figure it out. *Thinking face.*

Needless-to-say, I was placed in the same situation with respect to buying a file cabinet. Remembering what occurred some years earlier with my predecessor, I emailed this same Office Manager and asked her to provide me with the correct budget code given the similarity between the two codes. After some time, like hours, went by she finally responded to my email. I could tell that their plan to harm me was being frustrated. Her entire energy towards me continued to change and she wouldn't speak to me for days after that. She began to exhibit a fiery anger towards me and was bent on "getting me." My colleagues would often say that they never saw the Office Manager in the office as much as she had been. Prior to my employment, apparently, she would stay out of the office weeks at a time. Now she was in the office every day. Because I became a permanent worker, was in school completing my bachelor's degree and just going about my business, I became a target of her lies and attacks.

I have learned that *perspective* is a powerful emotion. However, during that time I was not concerned with her perspective of me. I was too busy being a single mother, completing my degree and looking for ways to advance my career by taking exams and possibly going to another agency.

One of the many lessons that I learned is that people will be fighting with you, and you may not know that you are in a fight. *Shrug emoji.*

Divide and conquer have been the "familiar" weapon used, especially among African Americans. Senior Management, especially our white counterparts, were always able to identify the weak link or the snake in the grass who was willing to sell out his fellow African American brother or sister for a morsel of bread. They would incite greed, jealousy, or suspicions to begin to bring about division. The obvious reasons for selling someone out was for approval, acceptance, and advancement.

Self-hating and self-absorbed individuals who were blinded by greed and refused to embrace or at the very least acknowledge how their participation with the wickedness in high places was deadly and devastating to someone. Anytime someone in authority or leadership can sleep or laugh when purposely setting someone up to fail, call the news media to report the matter, have the person removed from office or have someone moved from one side of the floor into an office back onto an open floor space and laugh. It's wickedness in high places. And it has been allowed.

I believe most leaders within local government lose sight that their behavior impacts the performance of the organization. But they will highlight the behavior of those who do not have authority or influence. What does that sound like to you? You tell me.

Because of the many things that I felt were unjust, I exercised my "rights" as an employee. Therefore, the mail clerk, an African American male, was chosen to spy on me and report to my supervisor everything that I was doing. He was being used to provide my supervisor with any information that would get me into trouble and bring me down. I honestly did not fully recognize what he was doing until I started writing this memoir. Again, my focus was my daughter, school and moving on from that agency. In retrospect, I guess I was compartmentalizing the stress.

I purchased everything from pencils to furniture to furnish conference rooms for the attorneys and after a couple of years an exam for purchasing agents came out, so I filed, paid for and took the exam. It was an education and experience exam, so I put down exactly what my functions were. My exam was rejected. However, I had the option to appeal the decision. Again, the veterans informed me that I had to use certain clauses, phrases, and buzzwords that the oversight agency was looking for. Therefore, I resubmitted my exam with the necessary revisions.

My Procurement Analyst exam was accepted. I was placed on the list to be "picked-up" at the agency where I have been working for a few years as they did in the past with the Secretary exam/title. But this time it was a little different. The General Counsel at that time abruptly quit-like came in that day, called people on their individual phone lines to say goodbye. Needless-to-say, we were all stunned and taken aback. It was a legal office without a General Counsel. My supervisor and I had to go upstairs to another division to discuss any issues while they were seeking to hire a replacement. It was crazy. *Smirky smiley face.*

I was waiting for the agency to reach my list number and to be picked-up off the list. However, my supervisor did not want me to be picked up off the list. I had to go to my union and file a claim that I was working out of title as a Secretary but working full-time as a purchasing agent. I ended up going to the EEO Office—that was a joke. and filed a discrimination complaint. Here goes all the union, legal mess—bluh, bluh, bluh. My complaint went nowhere but it was a clear indication that it was time for me to leave and this exam and being placed on the Procurement Analyst list was my ticket out.

I remember one attorney had a bad body odor. People complained to her and to those in authority about this attorney's body odor and whenever someone said anything to her about her odor, she would curse them out—loudly and badly—hilarious. However, some of my colleagues asked me to tell her that she had a body odor because I had a good relationship with her.

I told them "the devil is a liar and I will do no such thing."
...*wth*.

I had my own issues with the ongoing attempts to sabotage my work, the misinformation regarding funding available to procure, the staffs missing timecards, a staff member who had a wall full of pictures of his favorite rap artist whom he was intimately acquainted with suddenly disappeared and he came to me furious and almost on the brink of tears and all the other crazy stuff. So to tell someone that they had bad body odor was not on my agenda.

I found out sometime later that the mail clerk was telling people that I was a lesbian-which was totally false. But this is how envy works. However, I would be vindicated on so many levels about his remark because he was suspended without pay, had to take a sexual harassment course and was written up because of his gross behavior.

WHAT SHOULD HAVE HAPPENED?

What should have happened is that whenever my supervisor made unnecessary demands such as generating a report to track our expenses senior management should have reviewed the city's tracking system and saw for themselves that it had the same information that was being requested of me while also taking into consideration that I was the only person in the office doing purchasing for over sixty attorneys and realize that my supervisor's request was unnecessary. Although I tried to tell the First Deputy that an automatic tracking system was already in place and each time I would send in a request for a vendor to be paid, I had to complete a form with specific budget codes that were assigned solely to our district and department. Therefore, before a check could be cut for a vendor to be paid, these budget codes along with the vendor's name must be put into the computer system so that the Central Business Office (the office that processes all payments) will know where the money is allocated to pay a vendor. Checks cannot be processed and cut without this information–the system will not allow it. The tracking system that my supervisor requested of me, was the same information and she too had access to the tracking just as I did. In fact, the government's tracking system gave additional screens to follow for budget managers (as she was); it gave more detailed information than I could ever give and it was user friendly. But again, my supervisor was pushing me to do this tracking because she knew that she could get away with it. She was intentionally burdening me and assigning me tasks which she knew would be difficult to manage.

Also, the First Deputy, my supervisor's supervisor, should have required my supervisor to provide me with a note or send me an email notifying me that she had removed my files without my having to take it to the General Counsel and without my having to email my supervisor whenever a file was missing without any notification.

But because the First Deputy would not correct my supervisor she was able to abuse her power regularly and senior management failed us and the agency as a result because they were aware of my supervisor's past with having my predecessor fired-but again nothing was done and her abuse of power continued.

I think the General Counsel and the First Deputy could have handled the staff attorney's promotion differently. They should have transferred the former supervisor's out of the office first and then promoted the staff attorney or at the very least announce that these changes were taking place to somewhat save face for the former supervisor. As a result of how this situation was handled, the newly appointed Deputy was emboldened to abuse his authority right out the gate.

In my school paper, I further touched upon police brutality —Amadou DiAello and Abner Louima were the biggest cases during that time. I also mentioned that some parents wrongly use their authority over their children. But that's a whole other subject.

I realized that when people are given authority, and their authority goes unchecked or unchallenged is when the abuse occurs. When too much liberty is given to "trusted employees" this is what happens.

I believe that for public and private sector workplaces to be effective all sides of a story must be seriously considered--despite their titles. Additionally, sole credence should not be given to supervisors, vice presidents and presidents over the word of their subordinates especially if the supervisors, etc have a consistent checkered past.

The effects that misused power have on people in the workplace are destructive thus producing disgruntled and unhappy employees. It also provokes and increases hostility and often confrontation. Consequently, one may often hear one of their "disgruntled" co-workers threatening to go "postal" in the office. Such statements strongly imply that something is terribly wrong with middle and upper management in the workplace that need to be addressed.

When employees are left feeling as though they have no other form of recourse to express their displeasures and they're left fending for themselves it pushes people to a very dangerous level. The levels of attempt of murder, in fact, sometimes even murder.

I believe that management needs to seriously listen to and consider the cries and complaints of their employees and not solely hear the side of the supervisor or managers.

WHAT ABUSE OF POWER ACTUALLY IS?

The misuse of the authority vested in a person or an official for personal advantage or misusing it towards juniors or subordinates or a combination of both which results in adverse effects and breeds negativity is called abuse of power. Before understanding the abuse of power, let us first understand what exactly power in the workplace is. Power is bestowed on employees of an organization and power as it percolates down the hierarchy. This is the reason why the delegation of authority can stop the abuse of power in some cases. Power is a byproduct of power. Once a person is given authority, that person automatically has the power and can use that power in any way. The dictionary meaning of abuse is to use something in a wrong or harmful way or treating someone in such a way which is not acceptable by the law.

Similarly, abuse of power takes place when a person in authority exercises the wrong use of their power to the point where it becomes an unlawful act for personal gain or other reasons. Abuse of power at the workplace is also referred to as "malfeasance." All abuse such as sexual abuse, negligence, physical abuse, etc. are considered abuse of power.

In an abusive workplace environment, employees are subjected to behaviors and actions by supervisors that adversely affect their ability to function effectively in their jobs. Abusive organizations may not be in violation of existing laws because they are not engaged in discrimination or workplace safety violations. Rather, workplace abuse is primarily emotional in nature and as such may be difficult to challenge legally.

In addition to abuse by managers/supervisors causing overwork, family issues and health-related concerns are adding to employee stress. Job overload, economic downturn, mergers, downsizing and the ability of managers to monitor individuals' job performance add more layers of insecurity. As workers worry about layoffs, they do so knowing that the new information technology allows their managers to track performance division-by-division, employee-by-employee, and with startling precision.

CAUSES OF WORKPLACE ABUSE

The causes of abuse in organizations are vast and immense. The abuse of employees could come from many angles. Sometimes, the things that are deemed impossible to be true by ordinary standards are the reality in the workplace. There is never a good time to lose a job. Nevertheless, employees do get terminated during the holiday season for reasons like plant closing, acquisitions, and mergers.

The environment of a workplace or a corporate culture could mean the difference between a conducive or abusive workplace. Where there exists a competitive organization structure, there are a few individuals who have the power to command. It is sometimes the structure of an organization and the mindset of those few individuals that lead to the creation of the "monster" known as [the] abusive organization.

Condoned by the structure of organizations, those few individuals will pursue and use their status and power to compensate for or secure their positions. The goal of those who have power is to attain personal well-being and comfort. Consequently, to achieve this comfort, these individuals popularly known as management, abuse their power as a way to get things accomplished. According to Bassman and London (1993), there are no standard guidelines for the treatment of subordinates abused by supervisors/managers in many firms. The pressure to preserve their respective positions in an organization may prompt these managers to abuse their subordinates (p. 18). However, the reasons managers are abusive may not stem from fear of losing their power alone but can also be triggered by personality disorders, job stress, and learned violence. Such managers will promote undeserving subordinates on the basis of nepotism while taking advantage of a company payoff for their private lives.

A manager who exhibits abusive behavior may have considerable self-confidence and some managerial skills to cover up this "gray" behavior. The benefits of abuse may also stem from personal gratification—that is, a manager may feel more in control and have an attitude of superiority. The abuse inflicted may take the form of public ridicule, disrespect, overwork, and over control. Sometimes a manager may get so stressful, the abuse may involve making poorly planned changes and unrealistic or unfair demands, such as forcing one subordinate to do another subordinate's work in addition to his or her own work. Showing favoritism by a manager creates the greatest obstruction in decision-making. Subordinates are dependent on their superiors for reward, work structure and job security. But showing favoritism by any superior will exclude some subordinates from opportunities for development and advancement. The means of achieving goals by a superior or manager is of prime importance, even if it leads to abuse of subordinates (Bassman & London, 1993, p. 18).

Work environments that require a seamless flow of operation such as in assembly plants, telemarketing, and brokerage firms are candidates for becoming abusive organizations. Many supervisors who manage such workplaces emphasize the policy of work first and workers' well-being thereafter. Supervisors seem to think that once workers are in the perimeter of the work zone, they are subject to control by management. For example, manufacturing plants are required to provide an appropriate number of toilet facilities based on the number of workers. However, the availability of such facilities does not guarantee their reasonable use by employees in certain workplaces (Linder, 1998, p. S3).

Restrictions on the use of toilets are often imposed on assembly lines and construction workers by supervisors. It is the culture of such organizations that many assembly line employees must work in a hostile environment. Many times, workers feel they must accept their work environment simply because if they leave the job, their next job could be the same or nearly identical to their current workplace experience. In such cases, workers seldom rebel and often comply.

Learned associations like stereotyping which is based on negative or positive sets of beliefs about a certain group have helped to sharpen the edges of abuse in organizations. Stereotyping often bears the shade of discrimination. There is no doubt in today's workplace that either stereotyping or discrimination persists in organizations. The existence of this behavior may not be intentionally pursued but it could still be present even within a respectable, well-known organization. An organization does not need to condone the act of worker abuse. However, just a minor unsupervised behavior carried out by a certain person is sufficient to create a hostile work environment. When such a breeding ground for hostile and abusive practices are not eliminated, a chain of abusive incidents will evolve.

The source of discrimination in an organization sometimes comes from the most influential unit, Human Resources. Discrimination by human resource professionals takes many forms such as unfair application of policies, ambush of workers, and unchecked personnel actions by supervisors. Organizational policies sometimes overlook certain groups of workers while claiming to protect others. Hence, such bias in the workplace unintentionally creates a hostile work environment (Wendt & Slonaker, 1992, p. 44). Policies such as promoting the hiring of job applicants at age 35 or under with less than 10 years of work experience, have profound adverse effects on employees over age 40 (Hundley, 1992, p. 74). This form of age discrimination tends to intimidate employees in the hope that they will find the workplace unbearable, and voluntarily leave their current employer.

Many managers recognize the activity of hazing at work. It involves the rite of passage for newly hired workers. Since this becomes part of a workplace norm or culture, hazing is "tolerated" by organizations as necessary for newcomers in order to be accepted by coworkers and superiors (Josefowitz & Gadon, 1998, p. 22).

Perhaps one of the most flagrant abuses is ambush against the disabled. Often an employer has already decided to discharge an employee but will wait for the right situation to use as the cause of termination (Wendt & Slonaker, 1992, p. 44). Whatever their source, each hostile encounter in some way constraints employees' options or threatens their control over important outcomes.

Today, many employers are known for their family-friendly orientation. Childcare, nursery, and insurance benefits are designed to ease family burdens. All these new approaches have helped raise employees' motivation at work. However, what is deemed friendly to some may be downright unfriendly to others who do not fit the mold.

Organizations that are family-friendly often require their single employees to cover up for parental-leave, sick-child care, and other family-only-employees "goodies." Single employees in these organizations are also asked to work overtime, make last minute transportation arrangements, and take additional assignments just because "they are single." So, when do "single" employees get their breaks? One might think that "single" employees might have greater chances for promotion since they have the flexibility to deal with unexpected work schedules and assignments. Well, one should think again because often, that is not always the case.

As Diane Harris (1995) has noted, the top management positions are often reserved for those who are married (p. 120). In this instance, not only do single employees have a larger share of late-night work schedules/shifts, but they also receive a lower share of promotions. Family-friendly policies should be defined as flexible policies, not special privileges (Brackin, 1996, p. 104). Balancing work and life should be a commitment for all members of an organization, not just for a certain group of employees. Furthermore, employees should be recognized for their performance and contributions, not for their marital status when making promotion/advancement decisions. Certain jobs require work accommodations that affect many single employees such as "managing" office romance. Some managers believe in regulating office romance. According to Michael Lawrence and Tracy Thornburg (1996), in the Boaden versus Department of Law Enforcement case, when a police trooper told her supervisor that she is engaged to another trooper who also worked on the same shift, the supervisor suggested a transfer before her marriage (p. 5). The rigid protocol of the police department in this situation is an example whereby a couple working in the same place is forced to change jobs or accept a transfer. Is it legitimate to make a work assignment/schedule based on an employee's marital status? While some organizations may have their own "marital protocol," it should not be used as a type of punishment if two employees do fall in love. Organizations should be helping their employees to attain prosperous lives, not punish them when they are planning to get married.

Sometimes work policies that require employees to be adaptable and flexible can create a hostile workplace. However, certain expectations that are being underlined as crucial to the development of an organization can be deemed hostile to female employees and executives. Take for example when a female student is working in a grocery store that requires her to smile and greet every customer that comes into the store. Although smiling and greeting are common and expected in a service work environment, some male customers can misinterpret them. In this situation, the female employee's behavior may invite undesirable encounters. Her employer has in effect created a hostile workplace for female workers. Rarely will an employer spot an employee being pursued by a customer while working, and it will be even harder for a female worker to approach her employer to voice a complaint. As we all know, the employer or organization that emphasizes customer service will almost always believe the customer "is always right." When such negligence occurs, the well-being of employees is discounted to achieve higher customer service and sales.

The incidents of abuse also happen at the top level of the organizational pyramid. "Being at the top is like playing a guessing game in the dark for many women," claims Diane Harris (1995, p. 120). The higher a person is in the organizational hierarchy, the more "chemistry/being part of a special club" is required to do a job. For many women, the lack of this so-called chemistry can translate into not having access to the thinking of top management.

Although some organizations do not specify performance quality in their job criteria, the pervasiveness of such standards exerts conformity on the part of employees. Also, the lack of criteria may crush hope and limit opportunity to succeed. Let us say there are a few women who conform and meet their organization performance quality standards.

Will they still have an equal chance to advance in the organization? The fact of the matter is that many women are afraid to change the corporate culture for fear of punishment. Even though a few women can prove themselves to be "corporate-worthy," those with children will continue to be discriminated against in their careers (Harris, 1995, p. 120). Perhaps the most well-known case of sexual harassment in today's context is the recent settlement of the Mitsubishi case. One of the most unique aspects of this case was the sexist attitude of male workers that were tolerated by management. Also, the solution that was given by the company was "retaliated terror against women who complained" (Annin & McCormick, 1997, p. 50). The case was settled with the payment of $34 million to the victims, and an effort of intense reform to change male workers' attitudes. However, Mitsubishi has yet to achieve its reform plan, but women remain afraid to complain when things get out of hand. Women continue to witness, "Other women [being] ostracized or threatened for speaking up" (Annin & McCormick, 1997, p. 52).

Sexual harassment not only happens to female workers. Male employees are sometimes overlooked by an organization's policies. For instance, a male employee may be fired simply because he failed to report tardiness. Male employees who fall short according to policies often do not receive counseling and a written warning because "only females get progressive discipline" to avoid sexual harassment cases (Wendt & Slonaker, 1992, p. 45). Perhaps like the pendulum that swings both ways, "bad bosses tend to be equal opportunity abusers" (Loeb, 1996, p. 3).

EXAMPLES OF ABUSE OF POWER AT THE WORKPLACE

- Harassing or bullying colleagues or subordinates.
- Asking for sexual favors from the employees or making inappropriate contact with employees.
- Asking staff to perform personal errands.
- Interfering and disturbing colleagues or employees and disturbing their ability to work efficiently.
- Forcing colleagues or subordinates to break the rules of the workplace.

Abuse of power or malfeasance is a serious offense and one can be removed from his position in the office, or other serious actions can be taken against the person based on the seriousness of the offense.

TYPES OF ABUSE OF POWER

The commonly held definition of abuse, which we use in all our training is "a pattern of behavior used by one person to gain and maintain power and control over another." One thing to note about that definition is that we are talking about a *pattern* of behavior, in other words, not just one incident. These behaviors can take on several different forms. Many people when they hear the word "abuse," think of physical violence. It's important to note that physical force is one means of power and control, and it is far from the only one. It's often not the first one an abuser will use. Below are six different types of abuse we discuss in our training with new volunteers or employees.

1. Physical

This is the type of abuse that many people think of when they hear the word 'abuse.' It can include punching, hitting, slapping, kicking, strangling, or physically restraining a partner against their will. It can also include driving recklessly or invading someone's physical space, and in any other way making someone feel physically unsafe.

2. Sexual

While sexual abuse can be a form of physical abuse, we put it in a category by itself because it can include both physical and non-physical components. It can involve rape or other forced sexual acts or withholding or using sex as a weapon. An abusive partner might also use sex to judge their partner and assign a value—in other words, criticizing or saying that someone isn't good enough at sex, OR that sex is the only thing they're good for. Because sex can be so loaded with emotional and cultural implications, there are any number of ways that the feelings around it can be uniquely used for power and control. It wasn't until 1993 that marital rape was illegal in all 50 states, so some people may still assume that sex is something a partner is entitled to, and not recognize it as a larger pattern of power and control.

3. Verbal/Emotional

As one survivor puts it, "My ex-husband used words like weapons; like shards of glass, cutting and slowly draining my life, until I had nearly none left. I didn't think I was abused because he didn't hit me-usually... I had begun to believe his awful lies—how worthless I was, how stupid, how ugly, and how no one would ever want me." Other survivors have pointed out that while the signs of physical abuse might be noticeable to a friend or family member, the effects of verbal/emotional abuse are harder to spot, and harder to prove. Emotional scars can often take longer to heal.

4. Mental/Psychological

Mental or psychological abuse happens when one partner, through a series of actions or words, wears away at the other's sense of mental well-being and health. It often involves making the victim doubt their own sanity. We've all heard of stories of abusers deliberately moving car keys (and in some cases, the whole car!) or a purse, dimming the lights, and flat-out denying that certain things had taken place. The result of this, especially over a sustained period—and often with the isolation that abusers also tend to use—is that the victim depends on the abuser more and more because they don't trust their own judgment. They also hesitate to tell anyone about the abuse they're experiencing, for fear they won't be believed. A participant in a support group said, "He (her husband) had called me crazy so many times, I was unsure if anyone would ever believe me about the abuse."

5. Financial/Economic

Because abuse is about power and control, an abuser will use any means necessary to maintain that control, and often that includes finances. Whether it is controlling all of the budgeting in the household and not letting the survivor have access to their own bank accounts or spending money or opening credit cards and running up debts in the survivor's name, or simply not letting the survivor have a job and earn their own money, this type of abuse is often a big reason why someone is unable to leave an abusive relationship. Many of the abuse survivors have problems with their credit, because of an abuser's past behavior. A bad credit history can affect one's ability to get an apartment, a job, a car loan, and any number of other things necessary for self-sufficiency.

6. Cultural/Identity

Cultural abuse happens when abusers use aspects of a victim's particular cultural identity to inflict suffering, or as a means of control. Not letting someone observe the dietary or dress customs of their faith, using racial slurs, threatening to 'out' someone as LGBTQ if their friends and family don't know, or isolating someone who doesn't speak the dominant language where they live—all of these are examples of cultural abuse.

An abusive relationship can include any or all these types of behaviors, sustained over a period of time and often escalating. If you or someone you care about is experiencing this and you want to talk to someone about your concerns try reaching out to your local church or clergy and any other organization that addresses domestic violence/abuse.

IMPACTS OF ABUSE OF POWER AT WORKPLACE

- Impact the workability of employees.
- An employee who is being abused finds it hard to concentrate on work.
- Create a stressed environment in the workplace.
- Waste of working hours.
- Loss of manpower. Employees who could not deal with abuse of power might leave the organization or can take extreme steps like committing suicide.

These are a few impacts of abuse of power, and the count of impacts may rise to a higher number; there is no proper protocol to deal with the abuse of power at the workplace. In the next section, you will learn what an employee should do if he or she is the victim of abuse of power and what management should do to avoid abuse of power at the workplace?

Workplace abuse can take the form of verbal or physical abuse or sexual harassment. Laws prohibit sexual harassment and some other forms of abuse, but employees may still feel compelled to stay silent for fear of losing their jobs. Victims of abuse can file complaints with their company's human resources department.

Humiliation

An abusive work environment can lead the abused person to feel humiliated, with a feeling of diminished significance. Not only can humiliation impact an employee's work performance, but the humiliated also suffer from increased levels of stress. Feelings of significance contribute to a person's overall sense of health and well-being, and so the sense of humiliation can erode an employee's sense of self-worth. Women and minorities often suffer more from humiliation than others, according to an article in the "William and Mary Journal of Women and the Law."

Depression

Depression resulting from an abusive work environment can lower a person's ability to concentrate as well as devalue an individual's sense of self-worth. At work, depression can lead to lower productivity. A person suffering from abuse-related depression may also call out of work more often if he does not want to face his abuser. On a more personal level, a depressed person may lose interest in activities he previously enjoyed and experience disruptions in sleep.

Anxiety

People with work-related anxiety generally do not excel as much as non-anxious people, according to a study conducted at the University of Michigan. Employers are less likely to award anxious workers with promotions, the study found. Anxiety can bleed into an employee's personal life and decrease overall life satisfaction. People can become irritable and suffer from sleep deprivation, which compounds existing symptoms. Anxious people must deal with a constant, underlying tension. Anxiety can also lead to depression.

Employer Impacts

From an employer's perspective, an abusive work environment can lead to low morale and a high turnover rate. High turnover rates often affect a business' success since long-time employees better know the company's services and understand its mission. An abusive work environment can also decrease employee loyalty. If an employee does not care about her employer, then she will not strive to work hard and please its customers. She/he will not take on new projects or think about ways to improve the business. Companies with high turnover rates must also marshal resources to find and train new employees instead of using those resources to continue growing and succeeding.

One of the other side effects of abuse of power is that it also causes health problems, poor attendance, and low morale. Abuse of power in the workplace also affects us in our personal lives as well because we tend to take the problems we have on the job at home.

MINIMIZE ABUSE OF POWER : MY SOLUTIONS

If I can offer a solution to solving the abuse of power in the workplace to senior management and human resources, I would suggest that issues be heard without prejudice or favoritism from both sides. Then if a fair decision cannot be made between a supervisor and a subordinate, people should be put on notice that both positions will be vacated if things don't change within a certain amount of time and then watch the behaviors. I'm certain a valued change would take place within the work environment.

I'm reminded of the Chester Barnard theory. Barnard, a scholar in the field of human relations school said, "......leadership affects workers' behavior and the organization's general performance. Barnard also said, "...leadership could not be exercised by those at the top of a hierarchy solely at their discretion. Rather, a leadership's effectiveness depends largely on the willingness of others (i.e., followers) to accept and respond to it."

Barnard further stated, "His main point was that followers can greatly influence the nature and effectiveness of leadership over them." "...whatever the amount of legal, political or organizational authority leaders possess, their operating authority is granted, in effect, by followers."

Chester Barnard believed that formal organizations are made up of informal groups. These informal groups evolve to become informal organizations. The group's beliefs and values establish the organizational culture and determine, to a large extent, formal acceptance of authority.

Acceptance Theory to Authority

Management theorist Chester Barnard believed organizations need to be both effective and efficient. Effective means meeting organizational goals in a timely way. Efficient, in his opinion, means the degree to which the organization can satisfy the motives of its employees. In other words, the organizational goals will be accomplished, and authority will be accepted when workers feel satisfied that their individual needs are being met. This is known as the acceptance theory of authority.

Acceptance theory of authority states that a manager's authority rests on workers' acceptance of his right to give orders and to expect compliance. Workers must believe that the manager can legitimately give orders and there is a legitimate expectation that the orders will be carried out. There are a few reasons for this expectation:

- Workers will be rewarded for compliance
- There will be discipline for non-compliance
- Workers respect the manager for his experience

INFORMAL AND FORMAL ORGANIZATIONS

Organizations are made up of groups of individual workers. Naturally, these individual workers form informal social groups that become the informal organization. The informal organization exists within a larger formal organization.

Formal organizations operate under a set of rules and policies designed to carry out the organizational purpose, like meeting financial and production goals. A formal management-employee relationship dictated by hierarchy exists. Workflows from top-management to workers through hierarchical channels.
Each department is staffed with a manager and a few salespeople. Managers assign tasks to employees, and it is expected that employees will complete the work. Some managers reward employees for accomplishing all their goals by giving them extra time off or an extra break. Other managers are less generous with rewards. Some even threaten punishment for a less-than-productive day.

The **informal organization** is structured much differently. It is the personal contacts and interactions between workers that form into small groups. These informal groups of workers form their own organization within the larger organization and have a powerful impact on the acceptance of formal authority.

After the completion of my report from the professor who declared that he does not give out A's because he doesn't believe in them. This was his statement to me: "This is the most original paper I have ever read. Thank you. A++."

As a psychology major, I had a chart of the personality traits which enabled me to put a label and handle on my supervisor's behavior. *She was bipolar, schizophrenic, manic-depressive and a liar.* She lied about everything and everyone–without cause. Her stories were never checked or investigated, I believe because she was white and whatever she said was the gospel. After all, how could I, an African American woman. question this white woman's authority? What she hated most is that although senior management did nothing to curb her behavior, the joy I would get was telling her exactly what she was doing and I would hit the nail on the head every time and she hated it. *Angry face emoji.*

THE PSYCHOLOGY OF POWER ABUSE

It's important to understand the psychology of abusers and their supporters. Workplace bullying is all too common, and it leaves a permanent negative impact on both the victim and the company's culture. Here's a look at the psychology behind power abuse —and why it persists.

Power abuse is an issue that most of us have experienced at some time, whether we acknowledge it publicly or not. Controversy and debate around this subject continue to gain ground and interest, especially in the workplace.

Abusive people gain and maintain power over their victim with controlling or coercive behavior, and proceed to subject that person to psychological, physical, sexual, or financial abuse. As we have seen from the media coverage of high-profile cases, abuse can go on for years, often ignored, and worse encouraged by those who surround the abuser. Inaction to stop abuse, is a form of abuse itself.

Understanding the psychology of abusers is important as well as understanding why it may continue and possibly even increase.

Psychological studies in behavioral trends indicate that narcissism is on the rise: "Approximately 70 percent of students today score higher on narcissist scales than 30 years ago."Research has found that narcissism inversely correlates to empathy. The higher the score on the scale of narcissism, the lower the empathy exhibited.

Why does it continue?

Victims of abuse are often stressed and confused about their situation. This confusion can block the person's confidence to report the issue, or they ignore it, thinking it will go away in time. It doesn't.

Often the channel to address the issue leads to the legal department, but law firms can be a breeding ground for bully protection. Those with money or positions of power often have greater access to lawyers. They can exhaust the victim's ability to afford legal support very quickly, and they know it. The power of abusers is that they are often able to control the legal outcomes.

As a result, these cases often go unreported, undetected, and unchallenged, because the victim feels that the threat of action could be worse than the original form of abuse. This creates a vicious cycle where the perpetrators feel that by getting away with the crime, they are empowered to continue their abusive behavior. It is believed within government agencies that all the agencies are bedfellows, including agencies that are required to oversee employee complaints. Therefore, the threat of abuse is magnified.

Silent supporters and 'group shun'

Abusers like to have support for their cause, and because of their social skills and positions of power that can often compound the issue by enrolling others in what I will call the "group shun." The group—made up of the abuser and those who are weak enough to fear that if they don't join in, they will be the next victims—acts as a pack to ostracize an individual. Bullies often seek to remain hidden behind a veil of secrecy and cowardice and try to influence others to join in to take part so that if detected the blame is removed from them through deflection of the behavior onto others, the group.

This issue is rarely addressed in bullying training programs in any depth. Often the individuals involved are not entirely sure what is going on. It can creep over time and because of its stealth nature, it can be hard to describe to others so that they can see it. Where this occurs, the individual may be paranoid or delusional, leading to a double whammy of victimization where they feel everyone else has deserted them.

When you see colleagues being shunned and ostracized by peers and organizational leaders, do not enable the abuser by being complicit in your silence, or support. The silent witness is as guilty as the perpetrators, allowing the psychological torture to continue. The enablers are perpetrators by accomplices. Cowardice and lack of courage remain the motivation for this. Remember, if the vicious cycle is not stopped, logic would say you may become the next victim.

What can we do about it?

Putting a stop to power abuse and bullying in the workplace means ensuring education and a system support at an organizational level. Simply having a policy in place doesn't always help: Where policies do exist, they are often ignored or ineffective. The

Vital Smarts report showed that only 7 percent of respondents know of someone who used the policy, and 6 percent say that it didn't work to stop the bully.

When regulation fails, we need to revert to character, and herein lies the ethical challenge.Character is borne out of moral virtue, courage, and honor. In this case we need to ensure we are building employees of character– those who have courage to stand up for others, and themselves, and courage from organizations to reward those who do.

The culture of an organization must have systems in place to encourage employees to be aware of behaviors or influence that may not be acceptable, as well as speak up about those behaviors. Organizational leaders, regulators and business schools need to step up, enforce policies, be aware and understand the implications and risks of what is going on in their own organizations and the liabilities that they face.Individuals need to show courage not to participate, to call out bad behavior, and when faced with the situation themselves, have the language to articulate what is going on clearly.

Character is an under taught and underrepresented ethical trait in our executive education programs. It is the foundation of good leadership. Bring back character, and the need for articles like this may diminish. It's my hope they do.

Coming back to my story, where do you go when you know that your supervisor is out to get you? Where do you really go as a government employee or just as an employee? The internal EEO divisions are connected to each other and do not serve the average lay person. The external EEO Departments are connected to the agency heads and often do not serve the average lay person. Therefore, what happens is that people will learn not to entrust themselves to these entities because they are

RARELY kept confidential. RARELY. The word corruption comes to mind or misuse of authority. But hey you figure it out. *Smirking Face. Upside-Down Face.*

So, to a large degree, you suffer in silence or explode. However, should you exhibit the latter, then you are labeled as a troublemaker or hard to get along with or difficult. When you just want someone to authentically listen to you, giving the impression that your concerns really matter.

Here are some thoughts or questions to think about.

1) Think about a belief you have about someone or something and question it.

2) Difficult situations have a way of revealing what's truly in your heart. Agree or disagree? Why?

3) I heard someone say that if your joints are stiff and immovable, so are your thoughts. What do you think?

What are your thoughts and questions about this chapter? Write it down and make it plain (Habakkuk 2:2-3)

_____

_____

_____

_____

_____

_____

_____

_____

_____

_____

CHAPTER 3
A FRESH START?

Finally, my list number was reachable for Procurement Analyst, and I was called to interview at a paramilitary agency. I was offered the job as a Procurement Analyst (Provisional) because I had to pass my one-year probationary period before I gained a permanent civil service title as a Procurement Analyst.

I graduated with my Bachelor of Arts degree with a concentration in Psychology.

A FRESH START?

You see, I realized that while at my previous agency, I was assigned any and all things purchasing because my supervisor did not want to do purchasing and she was hoping that I would fail. "....... forgetting those things which are behind and reaching forward to those things which are ahead...." Philippians 3:13.

Whew, a fresh start, a new beginning, a new title, more money...........

WHAT HAPPENED?

Transitioning from a fully civilian agency to a paramilitary agency was an organizational culture shock for me. I was not accustomed to working with armed and uniformed co-workers because I previously worked with attorneys and dealt with their demands. I was now working with people on the other side of the spectrum of law but with the attorneys there was room for negotiation but with these guys it was their way or no way, period, although we were in an office setting. Their disposition and mannerism were militant and I discovered very quickly how "cliquish" they were and how blatant office affairs between leadership and staff were.

Procurement positions were created and given to select non-civilian staff. So why am I bringing this up, because it impacted promotions or better positions for civilian staff. It was commonly known that if a position became available, it was already slotted for a non-civilian person, therefore many of the civilians did not bother applying for positions. For example, the senior manager's girlfriend, who was an officer, was given an office while her colleagues were out on the floor with the rest of us although we had the same responsibilities.

It was challenging working from a civilian agency to a non-civilian agency. Although most were nice, they had an overall roughness about them which I understand because of their job. Here I am the ultimate girly-girl, working in this environment. Ugh, the struggle was real. As a result of the overall roughness, they forgot to often say please or thank you. I once shouted, "does anyone say please or thank you around here"? The Assistant Commissioner got wind of what I said and emailed me and said that no one has to say please, thank you or good morning---we had words but after that became the best of friends. Was he a "yahoo" for saying that? Absolutely!

If you weren't an officer or a non-conformist by not compromising your principles you were a target for harassment. Office relationships between supervisors and staff were plentiful and various forms of sexual innuendos were present. So there were always issues going on in the office for no apparent reason. Most of the issues were about nothing. I believe issues were created to justify the non-civilians' purpose for being in the office rather than with the rabble rousers. Think about it.

Whenever I had to visit one of our facilities, I often felt that I was being solicited by men and women for sex. To which my only answer was, via my body language, was "No, thank you."

I was responsible for construction contracts, preparing the bids, getting legal approval, awarding the vendor and vetting the vendor.

The common threads in my experience with the city are jealousy, sabotage, conspiracy, undermining, lies, ganging up and betrayal. Although these elements may be evident within the private sector, these same elements were evident from one agency to another agency. This was confirmed with colleagues working from other agencies of whom I developed working relationships with. It appeared that there was no escape. Again, this is my experience.

The senior manager within the procurement division, an African American man, was moody, a sexist and a bully. He would pick on one woman in the office by yelling at her, micromanaging her every move-including the number of times she went to the ladies' room. She was a quiet and religious person who was a recluse and he would often make her cry. And there was nothing that could be done or there was nothing being done about it. It was overlooked as, "oh, you know how he is or that's just him." Again, unchecked behavior because of his position allowed the abuse to continue. It was sickening.

He would check the attendance sheet and if you didn't sign in immediately, he was at your desk, putting the clipboard in your face for your signature. There were times, especially during the winter months when you were loaded down with clothes, bags, etc. and you just wanted to go to your desk to put your things down and then come back to sign the attendance sheet. Nope, he wanted it done as soon as you walked through the door. He was power tripping.

POWER TRIPPING

Power tripping is when people advance their own interests at the expense of the common good. The power tripper benefits at the cost of others and the organization by taking advantage of the trust placed in them.

For example, if the boss uses the company expense account to fund a family trip to Maui, he is using his position to gain personally.

Whether it's financial gain, perks or an ego boost at another's expense, power tripping takes a toll. Staff withdraw and disengage when power tripping occurs. They feel disenchanted, angry and, in some cases, copy the behavior.

The pursuit and holding of power are as old as mankind. It pervades every part of our daily lives. As women working in business, the professions or academia we must constantly tune our personal antennae to remain alert to the subtle and inappropriate uses of power.

Acquiring the skills needed to respond to a power tripper is vital for anyone who wants to move their career forward as a leader. Awareness of this personality type will help you soften your knee-jerk response to those whose fragile egos rely on exerting their power. Learning how to respond properly may well be mutually beneficial for you and the person trying to make your life a misery. Being aware of and learning from these encounters can also improve your personal effectiveness in any given situation.

We all know that people use power more than rewards and threats to influence others into particular actions. They are using power tactics.

Anyone can be a power tripper. While it seems obvious that managers can power trip easily because they have more control, however staff can wield power too.

For instance, one worker felt powerful because she had a strong IT knowledge base. As an IT person, she used her knowledge and expertise to feel superior over others. As a result, she came across as arrogant, patronizing and condescending when interacting with colleagues.

The researchers, whose study appeared recently in the Journal of Applied Psychology, observed that workers with a low moral identity tend to power trip more than workers with a higher moral identity.

Moral identity refers to the degree to which one's self concept is tied to demonstrating values such as kindness, fairness, honesty, or helpfulness.

Individuals ascend to positions of leadership by exercising power in one of three ways:

1. **Persuasive power** is usually a result of your ability to make an emotional connection with others and, through this connection, manage to persuade their actions. Persuasive power reflects your charisma, or the ability to draw people to you.

2. **Erudite power** is gained through extensive knowledge of a particular subject or an area of expertise. Erudite power is usually based on the acknowledgement of your intellect and/or academic accomplishment. People are drawn to this type of leader because they are deemed learned in a particular area.

3. **Positional power** is based on your ability to control and have authority over others by virtue of hierarchical order. Positional power is most frequently observed in employment situations where there are levels of employees, from line staff through senior management. It may also be observed in politics where a person ascends to a position of authority through an election process or by appointment.

EFFECTIVE TACTICS FOR HANDLING A POWER TRIPPING BOSS

Do you work under a bully? The easiest way to answer this question is to check in on how you feel. If you feel intimidated, frustrated and dread going into the office because you are belittled, humiliated, ignored, and cut down, you are in a hostile work environment.

Typically, bosses who bully are under tremendous pressure, love control and feed off two things—emotional reaction and attention. They thrive on the power to manipulate others. Unfortunately, the toxic boss may produce success from inducing fear in their employees, but they will also prove to have a shorter shelf-life when it comes to long term success.

Just know that you're not alone. The number one reason people leave their job is because they don't like their boss. A toxic boss exists in nearly every work environment in America. A survey in 2017 by the Workplace Bullying Institute defined this sort of workplace emotional abuse as the "repeated mistreatment of an employee by one or more employees or boss; abusive conduct that is: threatening, humiliating, or intimidating, work sabotage, or verbal abuse."The survey found that:

- 61 percent of Americans are aware of the bullying that takes place in their workplace.
- 60 million Americans are affected by workplace bullying.
- Bosses comprise 61 percent of bullies.
- 65 percent of bullied employees lost their original jobs when they tried to stop the bullying.

Most importantly, nearly 40 percent of people targeted by a bully experience stress-related health problems including debilitating anxiety, panic attacks, and clinical depression (39 percent).

1. Shift your focus from your boss to your job

A bully is unlikely to change their behavior, so your first option is to work to change yours. Instead of focusing on the boss who is trying to intimidate you, focus only on the details and tasks of your role. You have direct control over your performance, so make sure you are focused on the right thing, which is your job not your boss.

The more emotional power you give your toxic boss, the more your boss will focus on you as a target. A bully is more interested in reading your vibe than analyzing your performance. If your boss never gets your eye contact, he/she never gets the invitation to come into your emotional space. When you focus solely on the tasks of your role you stop giving off the vibe of fear and anxiety over gaining approval from your boss.

2. Understand the bully

The boss who is a bully at his/her core is an insecure, manipulative person who throws tantrums. They are selfish and immature. Most of you would not put up with this type of behavior in your own children and should not tolerate this type of treatment from your boss.The problem is your boss has a significant amount of control over your position. For this reason, you cannot meet fire with fire.

Toxic bosses manipulate their demand-arsenal so rapidly that it makes it difficult to meet their expectations or correctly follow their direction. It is a good practice to take detailed notes with times, dates, and details of conversations you have had with your boss. This helps you stay on task. You will have evidence of what was said and requested, when and on what date, when your boss makes a move to gaslight you on what you think you're supposed to be doing. Keeping this log available helps you stay grounded in the facts and out of the fire of emotional drama.

These notes also keep your boss in check with the fear that you may report him/her to human resources. Taking notes allows you to stay organized and to call your toxic boss out on your terms.

3. Set silent limits

Body language is a great way to silently but effectively deal with a boss who is a bully. Turn your body away from your boss every chance you get. Always give your boss the side of your body or the back of your body. When you must be face-to-face with your boss, focus on lifting your chest and your chin. This posture gently but firmly communicates that you're open to talk and not intimidated.

Bullies love to see people cower. When your toxic boss aggressively comes after you it is natural to cower; this posture will take over immediately when under siege of emotions like shame or humiliation. When you focus on your body language you covertly give yourself the upper hand. Your toxic boss will pick up on you having a stronger vibe and they will naturally respond less aggressively. Body language is a more powerful communicator than words which the bully can turn around and use against you; body language cannot.

4. Set verbal limits

Analyze how your boss treats you from an objective place. Make a list of the facts. You will say less and get more accomplished when you approach your boss with facts and a strong physical posture. The more nervous we are the more we tend to talk. When you have facts, you will set better limits. You can stick to the facts without trying to convince your boss of anything or squeeze any empathy or understanding from him/her.

Knowledge is power and facts are the knowledge you need. You must let your boss know you will no longer tolerate the negative facts on your list in terms of how you're being treated. If your boss argues or starts acting out, leave the conversation and escalate to the person above your boss. Tell your boss that since he/she is unable to communicate rationally that you will be addressing your concerns elsewhere.

5. Build a network

It is important to keep in communication with other employees who are also targets of your boss's poor treatment. Encourage your coworkers to document dates, times and conversations they have with your boss. The more people involved in documenting the facts the stronger the case you give to human resources to intervene and possibly seek to further train or terminate your toxic boss. The more evidence that is brought into human resources from multiple people the clearer the pattern of abuse is to diagnose and treat.

6. Tell management and HR about the bully's behavior

Let your superiors and human resources know, through your documentation and meetings with your coworkers and boss, that you have done all you can do on your own to cope with and abate your boss's flagrantly abusive behavior. Explain the impact the bullying has had on your physical, emotional, and mental health along with how it has negatively impacted your work performance. File a formal complaint and allow human resources to instigate an investigation. In the meantime, you may need to take a paid leave to avoid even more abuse once your boss is made aware that he/she is being investigated, or if possible, continue to work as you always have and give your boss the chance to show some change or quietly seek other job opportunities outside of your current organization. It's important to note that there are always other job opportunities available and your notes may come in handy should your boss, depending on the structure of your organization, decide to interfere with your job references.

CONTROL ISSUES

Exerting influence over one's environment or the actions or behaviors of another person is sometimes used excessively by those who fear the unpredictable and ambiguous and they feel the need to prove themselves, or fear losing control. An incessant need for control may become overwhelming and exhausting, wreaking havoc on relationships, careers, and overall quality of life.

What Can Cause Control Issues?

Control is typically a reaction to the fear of losing control. People who struggle with the need to be in control often fear being at the mercy of others, and this fear may stem from traumatic events that left them feeling helpless and vulnerable. As a result, there are many who crave control in disproportionate and unhealthy ways. The experience of abuse or neglect, for example, can make people look for ways to regain control of their lives, and sometimes victims lash out at other people in their lives.

The need for control drives people to turn to the external world to find things they can control. They may be compelled to micromanage and orchestrate the actions and behaviors of others, or maintain rigid rules regarding routine, diet, or cleanliness and order. For instance, people who are physically or psychologically abusive inflict pain on loved ones in the form of ridicule, isolation, restrictions, or physical or sexual assault, because they themselves are in pain, though this pain is often deeply buried and unacknowledged.

As a result of this control issue, I've learned that this behavior can be extended to other areas of the controller's life such as neighbors, friends and family. The other issue with this is that at the office, you really do not have any other "real" recourse, because human resource is generally bedfellows with those in senior management, therefore reporting one's supervisor could quite possibly make matters worse.

Control issues may be related to:

- Traumatic or abusive life experiences
- A lack of trust
- Anxiety
- Fears of abandonment
- Low or damaged self-esteem
- A person's beliefs, values, and faith
- Perfectionism and the fear of failure
- Emotional sensitivity and the fear of experiencing painful emotions.

SYMPTOMS AND TYPES OF CONTROL ISSUES

There are a myriad ways in which people might attempt to control their environment, themselves, or others. People exert power over others in intimate relationships, workplace settings, families, and other social groups.

Examples of exerting control over others:

- Micromanagement
- Keeping a person from seeing or talking to loved ones or friends
- Gas lighting
- Dishonesty

- Over-protective or helicopter parenting
- Physical, sexual, or emotional abuse, bullying, or taunting.

Examples of controlling self or environment:

- Disordered eating
- Compulsive exercising
- Self-harm
- Substance abuse
- Compulsive arranging, tidying, or cleaning.

Someone who struggles with a need for control may experience shame, anxiety, stress, depression, and a host of other mental health concerns.

HOW TO DEAL WITH A CONTROL ISSUE AT WORK

When a struggle for control arises within the workplace, the conflict can cause stress in the parties involved, on a team or on an entire staff. Recognize the source of the conflict and take action that will empower the parties involved while achieving company goals. Control issues are psychological and derive from the basic human desire for respect and recognition. In the extreme, conflict in the workplace can become bullying. Display leadership in such situations by maintaining what is acceptable in your business and what is intolerable.

- Provide a safe environment in which each person feels free to discuss the issues. Meet individually with each person involved privately in your office. Evaluate each person's goals, concerns, and fears as they relate to the work issue.

- Exhibit leadership by clarifying what you consider appropriate language and behavior among coworkers, managers, and owners. Hold detractors accountable for crossing boundaries by confronting breaches of behavior immediately.
- Invite cooperative initiatives in the workplace. Dispel any temptation to micromanage employees.
- Let employees know that you are the head of the company and, ultimately, final decisions land on your desk. Explain, for example, that infractions become part of employees' personnel files and can be causes for termination, according to your judgment. Give employees freedom to offer solutions, suggest courses of action and provide respectful critique.
- Practice active listening with the people involved with an issue. Allow each person to speak without interruption. Restate what each person says to express understanding. Display willingness to set aside preconceived ideas and defensiveness.
- Provide constructive feedback. Empower the people involved by validating what they have done well and correctly.

After the senior manager's deputy left the agency, an attorney with no purchasing experience was hired-okay. He and I had a decent working relationship, but I could tell that he began to change because the senior manager was in his ear about whatever. So, every now and again the new deputy would try me or anyone else in the office. One day I was out of the office because I wasn't feeling well. He called me at home to ask me a question about something stupid. Well, that was the wrong thing to do. I blasted him.

He never called my home again whenever I was out.

There was some strife that started between the senior manager and his new deputy and the tables were beginning to change and the senior manager started targeting him. One day when I came into the office around 9am, there was an uproar in the office-the Deputy was fired via the telephone. I mean, he received a telephone call and was told that he was fired effective immediately. *Cry Laughing emoji face.*

Of course, he filed a lawsuit against the agency and lost, because everybody he thought was cool with him actually lied on him. *Cry Laughing emoji face*

The moral of the story here is that don't take on other people's enemies if they haven't done anything to you.

Because the senior manager thought that he was part of the boys' club and that he had arrived, he behaved any which way he wanted-well something happened. I never got the full story but eventually he was demoted and somebody else came in and took over his responsibilities. He tried to leave the agency by way of applying for other jobs–but to no avail. We were able to see his downfall. I am not sure if he even had an office title. He was just known by his name-that was it. *Cry Laughing emoji face.*

I'm a firm believer that when people know that you're doing something wrong and no one is saying anything, it's because when they're ready they will use those indiscretions against you-as they did with the senior manager.

So, *the powers that be* transferred over this white guy with little to no procurement experience and made him a director. However, he was not to report to the former senior manager, as he normally would because it was the procurement unit, but to the Assistant Commissioner. By the way, the Assistant Commissioner was the former senior manager's supervisor. It was a trip and so was the new director. He came to the office like a bulldozer, throwing his weight around and he got into an argument with one of the analysts and offered to fight him right there in the office. *Shock emoji face. Cry Laughing emoji face.*

So now because the former senior manager did not have a title or any authority, I took full advantage of that. So, he and I would get into it because I totally disregarded him, was I right for behaving like that, no but it felt good because he was just a jerk. One day his boss came over to the office and held an impromptu meeting and was speaking generally about people's behavior and so forth, but I knew instinctively that he was talking about me because when he said that he expects the office to run like a well-oiled machine he looked directly at me. So, when it was over, I caught him by the elevator and asked if he would transfer me over to his office and he did. Effective immediately, I was to report to his office that next workday. Ironically, the fallen senior manager did not want me to go but wanted me to stay. But I left anyway.

I reported to my new location as agreed the following workday which was on a Monday. I reported to an African American woman and although I got the "411" on her I was determined to make the relationship work. I supervised two units, registered for school to get my master's degree and moved into a new house.

Unbeknownst to me, I walked into a war room. She had these arch enemies that she wanted to become my arch enemies. But that's not how I operate—here we go. I would hold staff meetings and would bring donuts and coffee because it was in the morning. I worked hard at developing a good relationship with my staff, but someone whispered to me one day that I stole my supervisor's shine. That was not my intention, nor did that ever enter my mind. I do not recall if I informed my supervisor about the meetings, but I would like to think that I did. She was out of the office a lot tending to a sick parent.

I had to fight often with one of my staff persons because she would not use emails as she was afraid of them. I fought with her, wrote her up, and she at one point called me an animal. But that did not stop me. However when I left the agency, she was an expert in using emails and was the first person to buy me flowers on my last day. She thanked me for everything-including the fights because she realized that I was trying to help her overcome her fears.

In retrospect, I guess I did steal my supervisor's shine unbeknownst to me. I could have been a lot more forthcoming and less controlling, but I was not thinking about it like that at that time. I thought that I was just doing my job.

WHAT SHOULD HAVE HAPPENED?

Sometimes when life hits us below the belt or has such a negative impact on our lives we have to find the strength and courage to fight back and stand up for ourselves. I believe the senior manager continuously picked on his secretary because she was "religious" and was a recluse but I believe that had she stood up to his bullying tactics he would have left her alone or at the very least thought twice or three times before he started his abusive ways. Yes, she should have made a formal complaint which may have supported her fighting back. However, senior management was aware of his abusive and bullying tactics and they did not correct him to stop the abuse.

Although, I must confess, the deputy's termination was hilarious on some level because of how it was handled. However, he should have taken the time to get to know the staff individually rather than listening to the senior manager and acting on that side of the story, therefore we laughed at him. Be mindful of taking on someone's elses' enemies because there are three sides to every story, there's one side of the story, then there's the other side of the story and then there's the truth.

But the former deputy found out very quickly that he was on the wrong side *of the law-if you will* when he filed a lawsuit, they rallied against him and he lost the case which was short-lived like his employment with us.

What should have happened for me, I'm not quite sure but perhaps I should not have fought fire with fire. Perhaps I should not have disregarded the former manager when he was demoted but he was such a *yahoo* and I thought it was good for him and in hindsight I should have been more forthcoming with my new supervisor whenever I was having meetings with my staff, etc. I've learned after the fact that if your supervisor wants to know everything that you're doing, you should shove it down their throats-tell them everything including when you're going to the restroom. *Smirky smiley face.*

72 • WORKING FOR THE CITY

What are your thoughts and questions about this chapter? Write it down and make it plain (Habakkuk 2:2-3)

Here are some thoughts or questions to think about. Write them down.

1. *F*alse _____

_____

_____

*E*vidence _____

_____

_____

*A*ppearing _____

_____

_____

*R*eal _____

_____

_____

2. What are your false evidences that appear real?

_____

_____

_____

_____

3. *It does not pay to be nasty and unkind to people when you have the power to be otherwise.*

_____

_____

_____

_____

4. *I could have handled things differently, but I was unaware of my actions. However, I did see everyone else's.*

_____

_____

_____

_____

5. *Remove the plank out of your own eye and then you will see clearly to remove the speck from your brother's eye. (Matthew 7:5). Think about and write down the plank in your eye that needs to be removed.*

_____

_____

_____

_____

Personal Notes

Some years ago, while driving through Beverly Hills during a summer vacation with my daughter, I was agitated after receiving a call from a "potential" tenant-who seemed to be a bit much before he was approved for the apartment. After the call, my daughter and I talked about there having to be a better way to live, especially when reminiscing about our job stressors, annoyances while witnessing beautiful homes with succulent green lawns, cascading mansions with the maids' quarter, separate entrances to drop off packages, etc. We decided that there must be *something* other than a 9-5 and we needed to identify that *something* upon our return from vacation–which we did.

We researched, made calls, visits, and then launched into the beverage industry which is a multi-billion-dollar business but very competitive. The bumps, bruises of men not remembering our names and calling you "girls," were deciding factors when prayerfully selecting the right partnership.

Working on establishing our business lifted a level of stress from the 9-5 as we had something else to look forward to. We took out pension and 401k loans and were well-pleased with the initial finished product. However, given the large number of beverages we learned after the fact that modifications to our color scheme was required because of trademark issues. We were told early in the development of our product that it may take years for our business to get to a place where we could leave our 9-5 and they were right-we are still working on it but perseverance is key.

Funny note: Some years ago, during the renovation of my new neighbor's house, each time I walked by their contractor's would sing a chorus from *Golddigger by Kanye West and Jamie Foxx* which was, "I ain't sayin' she a gold digger but she ain't messin' with no broke nigga..." This went on until the renovation was completed. I never really paid any attention to it because I was so preoccupied with the renovation of my home-until the singing stopped then I heard the chorus ringing in my ear. I guess they sized me up and saw fit to associate me with that song. I never spoke to them....I guess they were right. My point is, what did they see in me that I did not see in myself? *Smirky smiley face.*

Keep your head up and review my lessons below. *Smirky smiley face.*

What are your thoughts and questions about this chapter? Write it down and make it plain (Habakkuk 2:2-3). Explore what others see in you that you don't see in yourself. For example, are you bossy but call it something else, etc.

_____

_____

_____

_____

_____

_____

_____

CHAPTER 4
THE PERSON WHO HIRES YOU

After working in agencies performing agency-wide procurement, I was introduced to citywide procurement. This was one of my best and worst times working as a government employee. It was a highly political environment with many twists and turns.

This is where, looking back, I wished that I had paused and calmly thought about my actions.

THE PERSON WHO HIRES YOU

"Often the person who hires you will hate you." T.D. Jakes

WHAT HAPPENED?

The administration at this agency was wrong on so many levels. Whenever we requested a personal day we had to disclose the purpose of the personal day, otherwise they would not approve our request. So the argument from the staff would be why should we tell you why we're requesting a personal day, that defeats the whole purpose of making such a request and the kicker was that if we called in and said we needed a personal day because something came up, we were still required to tell our supervisors why otherwise we would be docked for the day or we had to use our sick time.

We had to request vacation time months in advance and it was not approved until two weeks before you were hoping to go on vacation which was a constant fight with management. If you made reservations for your vacation and you did not receive approval, you would make multiple requests including emails, and you went on vacation anyway. They would dock you for the time you took off. There were so many complaints filed against them, and no one did anything about it.

We had a Deputy Commissioner, at that time, who would curse people out so loudly and so badly that we could hear her throughout the floor. She would curse her deputies out and she cursed like a sailor. I recall one summer day, I decided to stay after hours to finish some work and all of a sudden I heard this familiar voice, *again*, cursing, slamming things, and just carrying on. So, I looked around to see what was going on, it was the Deputy Commissioner and her two cronies egging her on in her foolishness. She was going into everyone's cubicle opening the overhead cabinets, desk drawers and slamming them shut. It was ridiculous. By the time she got to my cubicle, I was ready and the three of them just looked at me and said hello because I gave them the look of death.

The following day, people were written up and reprimanded for keeping sloppy desks, plants on their desks and whatever else they found *out of order* during their rumble through the office the night before. People were no longer allowed to have printers or plants on their desks. It was a mess.

We didn't have a lunchroom or an eating area, so there were two empty cubicles that no one ever used because they were off the beaten path. Let's say we used this area for about two weeks and apparently, *"the powers that be"* got wind of it and we were immediately notified that we were no longer allowed to use this space as an eating area. Now mind you, no one used these two cubicles, and they were tucked away from other cubicles. Anything that this administration could do to make one's life miserable-they did.

A new senior officer was hired to oversee the day-to-day purchasing functions. He was a nice guy. But senior management, especially one person in particular, would beat him up all the time because she said that he wasn't *mean* enough. Oh boy and when they found out that he was married to a woman of color, they just tortured him but they were equal opportunity abusers. They didn't care about your title, your skin color, your aliment, nothing. They were just crazy. It was three women running the shop and I'm telling you it was bad.

One day, an employee did not show up for work and he worked for the agency for well over twenty years and instead of calling him to see if he was okay, they marked him as AWOL(absent without leave). The next day, nothing again, no phone call or anything from this employee. A few days later, someone went to his house and found out that he had died in his apartment on the day that he was declared AWOL at work. To this day, I don't ever think they called his family members to find out what happened to him because when I would ask his colleagues, they didn't know-they didn't know anything. Senior management found out about his death through the information from his colleagues. Even to this day, Oh my God, I don't know how I made it through that mess.

As managers, we were learning a new software which was inoperable but we were able to login to where the logo was captured. Well, all the managers had to login everyday, print the page showing the logo, sign and date it and hand it to the "nice" senior manager for him to hand it over to someone in upper management. And if you didn't hand it in at a particular time you would get into trouble, meaning get yelled at. *Expressionless Face emoji.*

Although they were equal opportunity abusers, they did have their regular targets, one of whom was in senior management and they would just beat up on her without sufficient reason. You would often see her walking through the office red and flustered. We always knew that if someone was in trouble that week, somebody was going to be in trouble the following week. So, we just waited for our turn to be abused for that week and then we knew that at least we were off the hook for the rest of the month– hopefully. *Thinking Face…. Praying hands.*

When I mean trouble, it wasn't just being yelled at, it was not being allowed to take a day off without permission, no personal days, no emergencies days, no sick days unless you bought back a doctor's note, even if you were out for one day making it feel like kindergarten. The city allowed us at least three days of absence before a doctor's note was required. Not with these folks; you either presented a doctor's note or you would get docked for that day. Your work would not be reviewed despite deadlines and then you would get into trouble because the contract was not registered in a timely manner.

One of my colleagues was so traumatized that she was too afraid to go to the bathroom. So, she would pee on herself, in her chair, and would not get out of her chair unless she absolutely had to. Like going home. She would bring a change of pants so that she would change once the terrorist left for the day. But she worked there for at this agency for at least thirty years and would not leave. I think she was afraid of change. We would tell her all the time, get up and go to the bathroom. She would not because her supervisor was riding her tail for every little thing. I would often stay with her during the week and would sometimes come in on the weekends with her to complete unreasonable assignments. She wasn't allowed to stay after work or come in on the weekends unless a manager was going to be in the office.

They would give this one manager big time grief over childcare issues. She had to pick up her young child by 6pm from a childcare program which was close to the office. This meant that she had to leave on time which was 5pm to pick up her child. Well, they felt that because she was a manager she should stay later than her staff. There were times she had to call her husband to pick up the child where his office was located a distance from the childcare program. Once she brought the child to work for some reason, I think it was because she was leaving work early or the child had a half day and she picked up the child from school during her lunch break. Well, that was the wrong thing to do. All I remember is her going into the hell hole (the First Assistant Deputy Commissioner [FADC] Office), only to come out crying and taking her daughter home.

Remember, earlier on I said that people would sell other people out for approval, acceptance, and advancement. Well, this is exactly what my nemesis was all about. He was a snake. It was him (my nemesis) and the Assistant Deputy Commissioner who interviewed and hired me. We got along for a while but when I realized his character or lack thereof and how he was just deceitful just to be deceitful. Oh, did I mention that he was African American. After some time, I ended up reporting to him. "The terrorists" knew that they could use him to do their dirty work and he did. My work would often be missing documents that were imperative to a package or I would be called into a meeting without any notice and was expected to be aware of something that occurred months ago, given unrealistic deadlines and so forth.

The racial inequity practiced in that agency was repulsive on so many levels, they moved a senior person to an entry level position and reduced the salary from $200,000 to under $100,000. Thankfully a lawsuit was filed and the City lost. The genesis of this was that someone wanted her job who had no knowledge or experience in the position and they wanted to steal it, so they targeted this senior management position and stole her job by calling me as well as other director's to show them the process of developing a bid to contract registration. These were people working with the senior manager's supervisor. It was depressing, shocking, fearful leading to a massive emotional turmoil within the department.

Deal with depression and anxiety to become a person with High Self-Esteem

Depression is something which eliminates hope and energy from your mind and makes it difficult to take necessary steps to make yourself feel better. While deeply involved in depression, fear, and anxiety it is almost impossible to have control over your self-esteem. So, it is too necessary to overcome your fear and cope with depression to increase your self-esteem. Taking the first step is always hardest but to go through these emotions is something a person must do.

OVERCOME FEAR AND ANXIETY

Anxiety

Anxiety is the natural response the body gets to stress. It is a sense of fear or apprehension over what is to come. Going to a job interview or giving a speech on the first day of school will cause most people to feel anxious and afraid.

But if your anxiety feelings are extreme, last longer than six months and interfere with your life, you may get an anxiety disorder.

Fear

Fear is a feeling caused by perceived danger or threat that occurs in certain forms of organisms that causes changes in the functions of metabolism and organs and eventually changes in behavior, such as escaping, hiding, or freezing from perceived trauma.

Overcoming Anxiety

Anxiety for fear of being judged or rejected prevents people from expressing their thoughts and personalities. Therefore, people who are socially anxious and shy frequently feel falsely understood.

Some anxiety factors and building confidence are given below:

- Maintain Confident Body Language
- Socialize More
- Keep A Record of Your Interactions
- Reframe Mistakes as Positive Learning Opportunities
- Spend Time with Confident Friends
- Meditate
- Socialize With Everyone
- Make Plans and Invite People
- Practice Self-Amusement

Maintain Confident Body Language

Body language shows just what you feel for the people around you. People usually move unconsciously in ways that reflect their state of mind. You can also use confident body language purposefully to attract more confidence.

Your body produces typically neurotransmitters and hormones that will make you precisely feel the way you think you should. For instance, if you live in a stressful community and are always afraid, people will physically assault you. Your body will produce high levels of cortisol, adrenaline, and other hormones that will prepare your response to fight or flight. This is very common in small doses. It's very unhealthy, though, if you're always nervous.

Even if socially anxious people don't live in a stressful external environment, they still experience the same overactive response to stress because they perceive they need it. That interpretation will reflect the language of their body and their feelings. For fear of interruption, they will try to take up less space to become invisible, avoid eye contact, and speak fast.

However, people who feel socially confident do not think they are in any danger. They feel secure. Their body represents this in the substances they create, and in this posture, they feel comfortable to talk.

Some body language has a higher chance of being correlated with confidence. You trigger responses in the body by assuming these postures and ways of moving, which can only be triggered when you perceive your environment as safe.

Standing and sitting with a good posture, slow moves, raising your hands above your head, and other confident poses lower cortisol, the hormone of stress. The movements often increase the development of other neurotransmitters, such as dopamine and serotonin, generally associated with feeling good.

In practicing positive body language, you open your mind to the possibility of overcoming social anxiety and building confidence. Fixing your body language is, of course, just the first step. You should also consider some introspection in solving psychological problems, which may trigger socially anxious responses.

Socialize More

Try to find social happenings in your region and go by yourself if you can. It's normal for shy people to stick to a friend whenever they go out, but that just hinders your growth and strengthens your fear of socializing on your own.

You can also practice your relaxed body language during your attempts to gain social experience. Keep good eye contact, stand up straight, don't talk too quickly, speak at an audible volume, and remember to take a few long, deep breaths if you're ever feeling a bit stressed out. Seek not to have a goal in mind when you socialize, such as making a new friend, getting a date, or finding people who will give you significant reactions. Don't rely on outside results to feel good about yourself.

Be happy, instead, that you are enhancing your social skills and confidence. This is because if you focus on getting an inevitable outcome, like finding people who smile when you start a conversation, then it can make you very nervous when people don't laugh right away. It depends on the experience. You can then take a moment to reflect on your experiences when you go home.

Keep a Record of Your Interactions

Of course, you do not have to write down every interaction. But keep a record of the times you've had the opportunity to avoid an interaction, but in retrospect you feel instead that you should have faced your fear and have acted.

This will be a useful reminder of your success in overcoming social anxiety and building confidence. There's not even a lot of time you need to spend to do this.

After you come home from your social event every day, take 10 minutes to write down your thoughts about one or two interactions.

Take Big Leaps Out of Your Comfort Zone

Some of these might include asking for favors from friends or strangers, or talking to people you think are in a higher position than you.

Rate these fears to induce least to most anxiety. Now, get to face those fears.

Start and work your way up with the easiest to address. You may not believe you'll ever have the courage to face the appalling situations on your list at first. With experience, though, creed can easily change.

Reframe Mistakes as Positive Learning Opportunities

Some people are afraid to take the smallest step out of their comfort zone because they are so scared to make mistakes or get themselves embarrassed. They want to remain in their safe area, no matter how much it limits their life chances.

If any of the encounters are uncomfortable, do not find them to be flawed. Instead, see them as errors of opportunities for learning. Be proud of them as they show you how to improve yourself next time.

With more social experience, your self-esteem and trust will gradually grow.

Don't force yourself to please everybody that you meet. Accept the fact that not every contact leads to meeting new friends or even a friendly conversation.

Spend Time with Confident Friends

Motivational speaker Jim Rohn is well-known for saying, "You're the sum of the five people you're spending the most time with." This is often true in general. If you spend time with confident people, or at least people working to improve their confidence, then they will influence you to develop your social skills and encourage you. Spend time with people you admire who possess traits.

Meditate

Meditation is a technique that is widely used to treat symptoms related to anxiety. It helps to practice relaxation in anxiety-inducing situations while training yourself.

To get going, find a quiet, convenient spot. Sit down and shut your eyes. Be careful not to try to control your breathing.

Wandering during meditation is routine for the mind. Do not try to control your emotions, and do not feel bad for distracting yourself. Just let the thoughts come and go and then get your focus back to your breathing.

Picture one of the scenarios after a few minutes of this, which causes your social anxiety. Imagine how that situation will make you feel. Don't fight those sentiments. Learn to embrace them and face your fear, rather than run away.

Socialize With Everyone

Through socializing with everyone, you are opening yourself up to many more ways to conquer your social anxiety and build trust.

Instead of just talking to people you believe can give you meaning, speak to anyone: the disabled, grocery store workers, or anyone you feel is out of your social interest sphere.

You're less likely to have some form of ideal outcome or ulterior motive while interacting with these people. It can put pressure on you to succeed when you interact with people with some kind of goal in mind. But if you're less worried about the result of the encounter and just enjoy the moment, it's much more enjoyable for all involved.

Make Plans and Invite People

You can schedule some activities until you start facing your worries, talking to everyone, and spending time with comfortable new friends. People who are socially confident do not just sit around waiting for invitations, they are actively inviting people out.

Think of specific activities you'd enjoy with a group of friends. For example, it could be playing a sport or having a meal together. This will help you start taking a leadership role in social situations, and people start looking forward to the events you are planning.

Practice Self-Amusement

This can hinder self-expression when you are always worried about rejection. You might just be comfortable sharing comments that most people think they should embrace instead of expressing their real opinions or sense of humor.

You will notice that people with humor are often quite relaxed. They don't continuously filter everything they say. Instead, they are aware of something funny, and it comes out of their mouth instantly.

The truth is everybody's got this filter. Even the most confident people know certain things are best left unsaid. That is nothing more than politeness. Yet people with social anxieties have an overly reactive filter. We hold back much too much out of fear of being rejected.

Now that you conquer social anxiety, and spend time with more comfortable peers, you can re-adjust your filter's sensitivity level. It is time to finally start having fun and to say precisely what you want to say without too much concern about what other people are going to think.

Overcoming Fear

Often, when we think of fear, we see it as an emotion which we would rather avoid. It is a feeling that can be so paralyzing and frightening that it triggers our instincts automatically to survive. Unfortunately, behaviors that are not in alignment with moving us toward our dreams and business success can surface. That can cause us to sabotage our success if we let fear control us.

Here are some tips to overcome fear.

- Embrace your fear
- Watch out for instinctive reactions
- Treat every situation as though you had chosen it
- Be resourceful

- Be glad of opposition and criticism
- Make fear of failure work for you instead of against you
- Control your thoughts instead of letting them control you
- Learn to recognize your automatic fear responses
- Find the calm at the center of the storm

Embrace your fear

What if I told you there is a gift to your fear? We can build meaning through stress and pain. Without that, we are living a shallow life. Our anxiety can show us our growing edge, the place we start becoming our authentic selves. This way, when we see terror, we will approach it from a place of curiosity and perhaps even gratitude.

Watch out for your instinctive reactions.

Most people react in one of three ways when faced with fear: battle, flight, or freeze. If this is you, then, she says, you are merely responding to deep-rooted human instincts. The problem is that these impulses lead people to let all their decisions cause fear.

Treat every situation as though you had chosen it.

If you're a business leader or an entrepreneur, situations arise all too often. That's not what you want, and you haven't planned it but flip and train your human instinct to say that perhaps I planned this to learn something from it and about you. Psych yourself out to get to a more calm and positive mindset. However, in your calm moments, acknowledge the truth.

Be resourceful

Resourcefulness does not mean monetary wealth, but how creatively you work with what you have, how you tap into your network, and enable your imagination to address non-conventional circumstances and relationships creatively.

Be glad of opposition and criticism

Know that traditional thinkers can try to shoot you down if you're up to something different. You challenge the status quo by doing something genuinely new, and you may bring up fear or guilt in those who don't.

Make fear of failure work for you instead of against you.

If you are afraid of failure (like most of us), you can get that fear to benefit you by modifying your default meaning. Instead of seeing failure as the opposite of success, failure to me is to remain small and not take the risk of getting out of our comfort zones. Look at it this way, and your fear of failure may push you to try something new.

Control your thoughts instead of letting them control you

You can't control what's going on, but how you react can be controlled. When something evil happens, and we assign a negative meaning to it about ourselves, this is an example of a downward spiral. Let's say, for example, you've been trying for a long time to land a big project or company, and you're finally turned down. It doesn't mean your plan fails, or your idea isn't excellent. It probably doesn't have anything to do with you as a human, so don't do it for you. Don't over-analyze your next step in achieving your goal and think about it. No single person or opportunity is your only path to success.

Learn to recognize your automatic fear responses

Start recognizing and realizing how these reactions impact you, but also how they affect others. It won't be easy, One of the hardest things to see and confess to ourselves is who we are. **Similarly, the biggest lie we tell others and ourselves is, 'this is who I am,' as if we are a set and unchangeable personality.** Ultimately, we're all made up of many sub-personalities. Our job is to get to know all our selves, the positive aspects and the aspects that could use us. This is your path to development, transformation, and actively choose to act from a position of power and override your actions in defense of fear.

Find the calm at the center of the storm

Find your safe and balanced position inside yourself and live here as much as possible. This is a place of self-confidence, and therein lies a commitment to your long-term goal against the short-term ups and downs of business and life. If your well-being, stability, and satisfaction depend on external factors, your stress level will be too high to remain on the entrepreneurial road effectively for a very long time. Instead, try to stay unattached to external events, which will help you to stay the course and feel calm while you're doing it. You'll be able to make decisions for a greater good rather than just a short-term escape from stress.

Coping with Depression

Depression and low self-esteem often go hand in hand. Low self-esteem leaves people vulnerable to depression. Depression stifles self-esteem. Depression often distorts thinking, making a person who is once confident feel insecure, negative and self-looking, past positive or neutral thoughts become *I am incompetent, I suck at everything,* or *I hate myself.* On the other hand, high self-esteem is associated with certain positive cognitions or beliefs, such as *I am right, I am a success, I am valuable to others.* While low self-esteem is associated with specific positive cognitions or beliefs, such as *I am right,* you can participate in an activity every day which improves your self-esteem. Below are some ideas on improving self-esteem.

Deal with dysfunctional thinking.

Research shows that the linchpin responsible for setting off low self-esteem is negative thinking. Depression is coloring life too dark. Depression corrodes forms of judgment and feeling. Negative thoughts are becoming destructive, making you susceptible to poor decisions and situations of abuse.

It's essential to tackle these corrosive cognitions. A valuable strategy is to research for accuracy in your thoughts.

Studies suggested that such three questions be asked:

- What evidence supports my thinking?
- Would others say this is true about me?
- Does feeling this way make me feel good about myself or bad about myself?"

That also involves replacing positive thoughts with negative thoughts. But this is not to echo empty statements. Instead, it is about the creation and use of genuine and meaningful self-expression. The reality is that all have strengths and weaknesses. To have good self-esteem implies to recognize and to respect all your hands.

Journal.

Maintaining negative thoughts in your head just makes them more prominent. Journalizing on these ideas brings them down to their scale. It also allows you to see the good things in your life that do happen.

Therefore, besides listing the negative thoughts, it is suggested that you record the positive aspects of your life, such as your health or loved ones. For example, for every negative thought that you record, please note something positive next to it.

Seek positive support.

Surround yourself with people celebrating your strengths and not your faults. Doing so not only feels good but also helps to strengthen positive thinking.

Create visual cues.

Visual signals offer perspective and help curb negative self-talk. Leaving positive notes around your home and office, for example, and keeping inspiring quotes on your desktop.

Begin the day with a boost.

Find uplifting and inspiring books, calendars, and websites. Or begin the day with a dose of laughter. These everyday gestures are a different way of creating a supportive environment.

Soothe yourself.

Researchers emphasize the importance of nurturing yourself, even if that is the last thing you think you deserve or want to do. (That's really when it's particularly vital.) Feed your mind, body, and soul in ways that make you feel special. There's no need to be grand (and overwhelming) in these ways. For instance, you might carve out some quiet time in your day. You could enjoy simple comforts like a hot cup of coffee, a lovely song, or a colorful sunset. Or maybe you are celebrating what you already have and not what you want.

Discover and pursue your passions.

It's easy to overlook your interests when you're down, and your self-esteem feels like it's sinking every day. It is important that you take the time to write a list of things that you used to want to do and stop doing, along with some things that you always wanted to do but have not yet done.

Redefine failure and keep trying.

It is common to think of yourself as a complete and utter failure when you have low self-esteem. Yet failure is a success story. Performance doesn't describe you as an individual or your self-worth.

There are countless accounts of persevering men, despite having to face numerous rejections. Think of any writer, scholar, performer, or artist. Everyone has at various points in their lives faced rejection.

There is no guarantee that you will get positive feedback from everything you do. All you need is one evidence of progress. Getting to one college out of 10, for example, still makes you a success. In other words, focus on and carry on with the positive feedback.

It's not easy to strengthen your self-esteem when you think your self-esteem is shattered but meet with a therapist to back it up. Feeling good about yourself is never too late.

A person with low self-esteem may be at risk for a depressive episode, but their concerns about self-esteem do not necessarily mean that they are depressed at the moment. Effective detection is vitally important for both self-esteem and depressive symptoms. A proper diagnosis and preventive treatment can lower the severity of a person's depression course.

STRESS MANAGEMENT

Why is it so important to manage stress?

If you are dealing with high-stress levels, you're putting your whole well-being at risk. Stress causes havoc to your emotional balance, as well as to your physical health. It narrows your ability to think clearly, work well, and enjoy life. It might sound like you can't do anything about stress. The bills won't stop coming, there will never be more hours in the day, and there will always be demanding responsibilities for your work and family. But you have much more power than you'd expect.

Effective stress management helps you break your life's stressors so that you can be happier, healthier, and more productive. The goal is a healthy life, with time for work, relationships, relaxation, and fun—and the ability to stand up under pressure and tackle head-on challenges. Yet managing stress isn't one-size-fits-all. That's why experimenting and finding out what works best for you is essential.

The following tips on how to relieve stress will help.

Identify the sources of stress in your life.

Managing stress begins by finding the causes of stress in your life. It's not as simple as it sounds. While identifying significant stressors such as changing jobs, moving, or going through a divorce is not easy, it may be more complicated to locate the sources of chronic stress. It's all too easy to overlook how your own emotions, perceptions, and actions lead to your daily stress levels. Of course, you may think you're always worried about work deadlines, but perhaps it's your procrastination that causes stress, rather than the actual job demands.

To identify your accurate sources of stress, look closely at your habits, attitude, and excuses:

- Do you explain away importance as temporary ("I just have a million things going on right now") even though you can't remember the last time you took a breather?
- Do you define stress as an integral part of your work or home life ("Things are always crazy around here") or as a part of your personality ("I have a lot of nervous energy, that's all")?
- Do you blame your stress on other people or outside events, or view it as entirely usual and unexceptional?

Until you accept responsibility for the role you play in creating or maintaining it, your stress level will remain outside your control.

PRACTICE THE 4 A'S OF STRESS MANAGEMENT

While stress is an automatic response from our nervous system, some stressors occur at predictable times: for example, a commute to our work, a meeting with the boss, or family reunions. When faced with such repetitive stressors, we can either change the situation or alter our response. It's helpful to think about the four A's when deciding which option to choose in any given scenario: **avoid, alter, adapt,** or **accept.**

Get moving

The last thing we probably feel like doing when we're stressed is getting up and exercising. But physical activity is a massive reliever of stress— and we need not be an athlete or spend hours in a gym to experience the benefits. Exercise releases endorphins, which make us feel good and can also serve as a valuable distraction from our everyday concerns.

While we're going to get the most from exercising regularly for 30 minutes or more, progressively building up our fitness level is fine. Even tiny things can add up in a day. The first step is to get up and be moving. Here are a few easy ways to include exercise in the daily schedule.

- Put on some music and dance around
- Go for a walk
- Cycling
- Use the stairs at home or work rather than an elevator
- Park the car in the farthest spot in the lot and walk the rest of the way
- Pair up with an exercise partner and encourage each other as we work out

While just about any form of physical activity can help to burn off stress and tension, rhythmic exercise is particularly useful. Walking, biking, swimming, dancing, spinning, tai chi, and aerobics are all excellent choices. But whatever you choose, make sure you enjoy it, so you're more likely to stick to it.

While you are moving, you are making a conscious effort to pay attention to your body and to the physical (and sometimes emotional) stimuli that you feel when you walk. For example, concentrate on coordinating your breathing with your movements, or notice how the air or sunlight on your skin feels. Adding this aspect of mindfulness will help you break out of the loop of negative thoughts, which often accompany overwhelming stress.

Connect to others

Nothing is more calming than spending quality time with another human being that makes us feel safe and understandable. Face-to-face interaction triggers a cascade of hormones that counteracts the body's defensive response to "fight-or-flight." Natural stress reliever of its kind (as a bonus it also helps to stave off depression and anxiety). And make it a point to communicate with family and friends frequently–and in person.

Keep in mind that we don't need to be able to fix our burden on the people we speak to. They just got to be good listeners. So, try not to let fears about appearing weak or being a burden deter us from opening up. The people who care for us will be flattered by our confidence. It just strengthens our connection.

Of course, having a pal close by to lean on when we feel overwhelmed by stress is not always realistic, but by building and maintaining a network of close friends, we can improve our resilience to the stressors of life.

Make time for fun and relaxation

You will be raising stress in your life beyond a take-charge approach and a positive attitude by clicking "me" time out. Don't get so caught in the hustle and bustle of life that you forget to look after your own needs. Nursing is a necessity, not a luxury.

When you regularly make time to have fun and relax, you'll be in a great place to handle the stressors of life.

Set aside leisure time.

Include relaxation in your daily schedule. Do not require encroachment on other obligations. This is your time to take a break and recharge your batteries from all commitments.

Do something you enjoy every day.

Whether it's stargazing, playing the piano, or working on your bike, make time for leisure activities that bring you joy.

Keep your sense of humor.

This requires the desire to self-laugh. The act of laughing helps your body in several ways to fight stress.

Take up a relaxation practice.

Relaxation techniques such as yoga, meditation, and deep breathing activate the body's response to relaxation, a state of restfulness that is the opposite of the reaction to combat or flight or stress mobilization. As you learn these techniques and practice them, your stress levels will decrease, and your mind and body will become calm and centered.

Manage your time better

Poor time management can cause considerable stress. It is hard to stay calm and focused when you're stretched too thin and running behind. Plus, you'll be tempted to stop or minimize all the good things you're supposed to do to keep stress in check, such as socializing and getting enough sleep. The good news: There are things you can do to strike a better balance between work and life.

Don't over-commit yourself.

You should not plan things back-to-back or attempt to cram too much into a single day. Perhaps too often we underestimate how long it will take for things to get done.

Prioritize tasks.

Make a list of the tasks you need to perform and address them in order of importance. First, do the high priority items. If you have something to do that is particularly unpleasant or frustrating, get it over with early. As a result, the remainder of your day will be more pleasant.

Break projects into small steps.

If a big project seems daunting, do a step-by-step plan. Reflect on one achievable step at a time, rather than thinking all at once.

Delegate responsibility.

You don't have to do it all by yourself, be it at home, at school, or work. If other people can attend to the task, why not let them? Let go of the wish to control or supervise every small step. In the process, you will be letting go of unnecessary stress.

Maintain balance with a healthy lifestyle

Aside from regular exercise, other healthy lifestyle choices can boost your stress resistance.

Eat a healthy diet.

Well-nourished bodies are better suited to coping with stress, so be conscious of what you eat. Start the day right with breakfast and keep your energy and mind clear throughout the day with healthy, nutritious meals.

Reduce caffeine and sugar.

Temporary "highs" of caffeine and sugar often lead to a mood and energy crash. By reducing your diet's amount of coffee, soft drinks, chocolate, and sugary snacks, you'll feel more relaxed and sleep better.

Avoid alcohol, cigarettes, and drugs.

Alcohol or drug self-medication can provide an easy way out of stress, but the relief is only temporary. Do not avoid the problem at hand or mask it, deal with problems head-on and with a clear mind.

Get enough sleep.

Adequate sleep is fueling the mind and body. Feeling tired can raise tension because it can trigger irrational thinking.

Learn to relieve stress at the moment

You need a way to manage your stress levels right now, when you're frazzled by your morning commute, trapped in a tense meeting at work, or fried out from another fight with your partner. This is where the relief from swift tension comes in.

The best way to reduce tension is to take a deep breath and use your senses—what you see, hear, taste, and touch—or through a gesture that is calming. You can quickly relax and focus yourself by viewing a favorite photo, smelling a specific scent, listening to a favorite piece of music, tasting a piece of gum, or hugging a pet, for example. Not everyone, of course, reacts equally to every sensory experience. The secret to quick relief from stress is exploring and finding the extraordinary sensory experiences that work best for you.

ANXIETY AND STRESS IN THE WORKPLACE

Having an anxiety disorder can have a major impact in the workplace. People may turn down a promotion or other opportunities because it involves travel or public speaking. People may make excuses to get out of office parties, staff lunches, meetings with coworkers or the inability to meet deadlines.

In a national survey on anxiety in the workplace, people with anxiety disorders commonly cited these as difficult situations: dealing with problems; setting and meeting deadlines; maintaining personal relationships; managing staff; participating in meetings, and making presentations.

Tell Your Employer?

It's your decision to tell your employer about your anxiety disorder. Some people do so because they need accommodations, others want to educate people about their condition, and some do not want to hide their illness.

Being qualified means you must satisfy an employer's requirements for the job and be able to perform essential functions on your own or with reasonable accommodation. An employer cannot refuse to hire you because your disability prevents you from performing duties that are not essential to the job.

Tips to Manage Stress and Anxiety at Work

Getting stressed out at work happens to everyone, and it's perfectly normal. But stress that is persistent, irrational, and overwhelming and impairs daily functioning may indicate an anxiety disorder.- Keep these ideas in mind to keep your work life manageable:

- *Work!* In addition to financial reasons, working can be important for your self-esteem and it adds to your social identity.
- *Tell a trusted coworker.* Knowing that someone accepts your condition can be comforting and it may reduce any anticipatory anxiety about having a panic attack at work.
- *Educate yourself.* Learn to recognize the symptoms of your disorder and how to handle them if you experience any panic attacks at work.
- *Practice time management.* Make to-do lists and prioritize your work. Schedule enough time to complete each task or project.
- *Plan and prepare.* Get started on major projects as early as possible. Set mini deadlines for yourself. Anticipate problems and work to prevent them.
- *Do it right the first time.* Spend the extra time at the outset and save yourself a headache later when you must redo your work.

- *Be realistic.* Don't over commit or offer to take on projects if you don't realistically have enough time.
- *Ask for help.* If you're feeling overwhelmed, ask a coworker for help. Later you can return the favor.
- *Communicate.* Speak up calmly and diplomatically if you have too much to handle. Your supervisor may not realize you're overextended.
- *Stay organized.* Filing and clearing your desk and computer desktop may rank low on your priority list, but they can save you time in the long run and may prevent a crisis later.
- *Avoid toxic coworkers.* Try to ignore negativity and gossip in your workplace.
- *Take breaks.* A walk around the block or a few minutes of deep breathing can help clear your head.
- *Set boundaries.* Try not to bring work home with you. Don't check your work e-mail or voice mail after hours.
- *Savor success.* Take a moment to celebrate your good work before moving on to the next project. Thank everyone who helped you.
- *Plan a vacation.* You'll be rejuvenated and ready to work when you come back.
- *Take advantage of employer resources and benefits.* Your workplace may offer an Employee Assistance Program (EAP), discounts to gyms, or skill-building courses. Learn what's available to you.
- *Be healthy.* Eat healthfully, get enough sleep, exercise regularly, and limit caffeine and alcohol. Try to keep your body and mind in shape to handle challenging situations.

One day, it was the wrong day to mess with me. I cursed out my supervisor, loudly, for about an hour to the point where the Assistant Commissioner of Security came upstairs to gently ask me to come downstairs to his office and talk about what happened. Of course, I did. So, he asked me to stay home for a few days to rest, which I did. So, they suggested that I go talk to someone and I did. I went to go see a psychiatrist and he prescribed medicine-I forgot what it was, but it was for anxiety. I think I took one and that was it. We were fierce enemies from that point on until I left the agency. He did everything in his power to ruin me, but it never worked.

So, things began to change in terms of senior management. A new Deputy Commissioner(DC) was hired because the previous DC who cursed people out was forced to leave the agency. But word on the street was that she was fired and ended up moving out of the State. This new DC was crazy too. He caught the FADC shredding some papers, he blasted her, moved her out of her office, demoted her and had her sit in an area where no one was sitting. He moved one of the other terrorists to a completely different department on another floor. He totally dismantled that terrorist group that was established in the office. But the new DC was the kind of person who would walk right by you and would not speak to you. He would be in the elevator with you and would not part his month. He would go to someone's desk and curse them out. He demoted people left and right. He demoted a director, had her sit in the area with the secretary which was outside of the *"nice guy's"* office -it was a damn mess.

One day as the DC was walking by, he saw a staff member sleeping at her desk. I mean head leaning back in the chair, mouth opened, the whole bit. He stood there for about two minutes just looking at her and turning beat red. He turned around and got the "nice guy" to wake her up and she was called into the office. *Crying laughing emoji face.*

This same woman would pluck her chin hairs every day at her desk. Everyday. My colleague and I would often ask each other, how many chin hairs does she have? After picking her chin hairs-she would run to the bathroom and because she waited so long to go she would often leave the bathroom stall door open leaving no imagination to the obvious....*SMH Emoji*

Some of the agency oversights began to realize that this new DC did not know what he was talking about regarding procurement and he made some seriously wrong decisions. He left before they fired him.

We lovingly worked with an attorney who was unorthodox to say the least. He was totally out of order. He would call us stupid monkeys and would label us "house" or "field." Which meant that we were either house niggas or field niggas and he would say it loudly in front of others and in the middle of the floor. Every day going to work with this guy was always going to be a riot. Oh, wait a minute did I mention that he was African?! We loved him because if anything went down, he was there to support us one hundred percent. He was the kind of person that you would want to have in your back pocket. *Smirky smiley face.* He helped me in every way he could. He protected me, even watched out for me when management was being crazy. He helped me to get a promotion and a salary increase. So, his foolery could have been taken the wrong way but because of his character and his willingness to help me and others like me- we loved him. We overlooked his foolishness and after a while you didn't hear his nonsense anymore.

Lastly, to add fuel to the fire regarding this place, we had to deal with a staff member who would often pass gas in meetings, walking by your desk, whenever and wherever and her response was, "it's a natural bodily function." *Smirky smiley face.*

ı

WHAT SHOULD HAVE HAPPENED?

I should have ran out of that place sooner than I did.

Write down your thoughts and questions about this chapter. Write it down and make it plain (Habakkuk 2:2-3)

CHAPTER 5
THE HEART IS DECEITFUL

As stated below in the bible verse, the heart is desperately wicked. This chapter addresses the bible school, church going staff person who coveted my position and thus teamed up with my immediate supervisor to try to bring me down. One would think that if you consult with your supervisor and accept their counsel that you *should* be okay. However, I came to realize that it was a set-up from the beginning.

THE HEART IS DECEITFUL

"How you gonna hire me and then want me to be stupid?" Bishop T.D. Jakes.

"The heart is deceitful above all things and desperately wicked-who can understand it?" Jeremiah 17:9

WHAT HAPPENED?

I was offered a middle management position at an agency that purchased medical supplies for the city. I negotiated for my salary and was counter offered significantly less and after some going back and forth, a stipulation was presented that I would receive a portion of the salary for one year and then I would get the remainder after one year. Given the insanity that was going on at my current agency, with my nemesis taking over my supervisor's position while she was out on medical leave as well as intermittent days of absence. Therefore, it was in my best interest to leave so I accepted the offer. With the city you can have an office title and a civil service title, which is a permanent title. Well I had a permanent civil service title that I served in for at least a year at my then former agency and senior management including Human Resources informed me that I could transfer my permanent title over to this new agency.

I was hired to oversee a unit with eight procurement professionals including two supervisors. As most of the staff worked together for years, the morale was extremely low to the point where they were not speaking to each other and the relationship between the two supervisors was particularly strained.

Being new to the agency of course I was given variations of the real issues. So, while learning the "ropes" of the agency, I learned that the staff was promised raises a few years before I was hired, I discussed this matter with my supervisor and of course her understanding or narration was different. Nevertheless, I persuaded my supervisor to consider salary increases for everyone. However, I had to show cause for this request, so I increased functions, gave promotions, restructured the unit, required weekly reports, hosted monthly meetings and required a continuing education schedule which was free of charge for most courses. After a while, I developed a persuasive argument for salary increases to be granted.

To continue the uptick of increased morale, I would bring in Dunkin' Donuts and coffee at least once a week. My staff was at the very least talking and laughing with each other and people outside of the unit would secretly tell me that whatever I did has worked because they haven't seen any interaction within my unit for a long time-so it was working.

Then one day while meeting with my supervisor, she said to me "it feels like you're having a party and I'm not invited." *Pause and calmly think about that.*

Not too long after that I received an email from a staff member that excluded her supervisor about her radio. *Question mark face.*

Now she and I *never* had a conversation about this radio or anything else. I could accept her email to me, but it was in all capital letters which meant that she was yelling at me. Apparently, the volume of this member's radio was an ongoing issue among the staff but I was unaware of it because each time I walked by her desk I could hardly hear the radio. Needless-to say, I was totally confused because this was the first time that I heard of this issue.

I showed my supervisor the email and she instructed me to write-up the staff member once I discussed the matter with the staffs' supervisor. Now keep in mind I'm still new trying to learn the ropes so I complied with my supervisor's directive. Unbeknownst to me, all of this was a part of a set-up and I'm sure some of you can relate. Let's continue. The staff members' supervisor and I discussed the write up and she appeared to have been in agreement with my actions, therefore the write-up was prepared, reviewed, and approved by my supervisor and I scheduled a time to meet with the staff person, her supervisor, presented the document and went through the process.

Ironically, the staff person did not understand why she was getting written up and she had never spoken to her supervisor about this radio issue. *Bizarre.* During the meeting, I noticed that her supervisor was curiously quiet during the meeting as if she wasn't in agreement with what I was doing although I previously discussed it with her. Needless-to-say, the staff member was not happy about the write-up but I informed her that it was not in her permanent personnel file and after 18 months, she could request to have the write up removed from her file. This was one of many incidents that my supervisor instructed me to do something and left me hanging with the mess.

A few weeks later I was informed that I couldn't use my permanent title because it was an agency promotional title. We went back and forth for a while on this and it was rather messy. This was my permanent title that I now had to consider giving up in lieu of another less desirable title or go back to my former agency-which wasn't an option. So, I settled for the less desirable title and I was not happy about that alllllllll!

A couple of months later, I was discreetly informed that my current agency picked-up several people from the list of 'permanent titles', that I had to give up—well that was the wrong thing for me to hear. Needless-to-say, it was on and popping *again* about my previous title of Administrative Manager, I received all kinds of excuses including the agency that oversees all the exams. It was a bunch of nonsense and I knew it, I said it but there wasn't anything that I could do about it. In hindsight, I still believe that my supervisor had a hand in keeping my original title off the table as an option. She was so afraid, from my assessment, that anything other than what she was accustomed to unnerved her-including a title that could give the appearance of equal to hers. I told her once that she reminded me of the book titled "Who Moved My Cheese" because she hated for her *cheese* to be moved and apparently, I was moving her cheese.

When I started there, my unit had seven people and 2 of them were supervisors. One for the small purchasing staff and the other was for administration. However, there was a love-hate relationship between them and I believed that the two of them were going to kill each other one day. Every day they came into my office complaining about each other. I'd purposed that if they were going to get into a fight, which seemed inevitable, I was going to call the head of security to have them both removed and suspended for two weeks without pay. Luckily, it didn't have to come to that. While meeting with my supervisor, I would openly discuss my frequent encounters with these two supervisors and I expressed my deep concerns about the constant friction between the two supervisors.

Because I expressed some concerns about these two supervisors potentially killing each other, my supervisor suggested that I remove one of the supervisors and become responsible for the role or reduce both their supervisory positions because "it was too top heavy." It was a conspiracy from the very beginning, unbeknownst to me. So, I removed the supervisory functions from one of the supervisors but I did not allow management to take money away from her or reduce her title-which they wanted to do. I took over the function as it allowed me to be directly involved with all the activities of that unit, rather than just signing off on things that I did not fully comprehend. This way, I would be totally involved, would understand the ins and outs of these procurements and thus would feel comfortable approving it. I gave the other supervisor a title change, an office title change and a salary increase which she stated was promised to her before I arrived but was never completed. The saga began. There was an influx of calls and emails from internal and external stakeholders informing me that purchase orders were not processed properly from the previous supervisor. So I had to address and resolve each matter which was not an easy task.

My supervisor, a current day "Karen," would often use trigger phrases like "I'm afraid" or "I'm scared" implying that I was doing one thing or another which was absolutely untrue.

Although her supervisor (the DC-Deputy Commissioner) and I had a good relationship, I stayed at her home, had lunch and dinner on the weekends. As a result of our relationship, I had hoped that the DC would have asked me if my supervisor's narrative or claim was correct or not. My supervisor made everything I did wrong and because the DC did not have any procurement experience or knowledge, she relied heavily on my supervisor. However, I believe that because they were both white women my supervisor's narrative of me emboldened her to sabotage my work. So she continued to overload me and my team with manufactured work in spite of my reporting that we were overloaded.

We were assigned tasks that were normally out of the "function" of my unit. My former supervisor began to meet privately with my assistant without any form of communication to me and began training my assistant in various types of procurements which gave the impression that she was being trained for my job-which she never got. Although I addressed this issue with my supervisor and her supervisor nothing was done which added a certain kind of strand between my assistant and me. I did realize however that this was a tactic to create strife and division within my group as my assistant of course started behaving differently towards me and the group. Which I believe was the goal. Therefore, I adapted to what was going on which disarmed them by not addressing the private meetings, and treated my assistant and supervisor as if everything was okay. After a while, it was okay and the training and meeting stopped. I did not give them my power or my peace. It was a defensive mechanism that I adopted throughout my tenure with the city and it worked.

My former supervisor was disproportionately focused on my unit therefore, no one was looking at her unit or their work. Whenever she was out of the office, I would oversee her unit and without fail I would receive calls or emails about issues with my supervisor's work being rejected by one of the oversights.

Documents were missing from the registration packages, therefore the oversight agency refused to register the contract. Her supervisor (the DC) was unaware of all these matters within the contracts unit which was one of the reasons why the focus stayed on my unit because I knew the truth about the work within the contract unit and she had to trash my unit's work to keep the focus on me.

If I bought morning refreshments for my unit which was openly displayed, my supervisor would quite often say to me that she felt as if we were having a party and she was not invited. Now keep in mind she oversaw the day-to-day functions of the contracts unit.

When I re-engineered my unit by moving one of the two supervisors to the contracts units, one of the actions that the DC wanted was to reduce the former supervisor's salary and she was only making $65,000. Of course, my answer was no, I was just transferring her to another unit which was a comparable position. You see, contracts in any agency were always considered a more elite form of procurement. One of the many lessons I learned was that senior management often targeted the "purse" when it involved people of color. However, whenever other ethnicities were being transferred or dealt with, their salaries were rarely impacted and whenever their salaries were reduced it was at a fraction compared to their African American colleagues. Although non-melanated colleagues made far more money, their salary reduction was a joke. For example, if a person of color was making $135,000, their salary could be reduced to $100,000, whereas their counterparts would make $150,000 (for the same position) and their salary could be reduced to $145,500. You figure it out.

I heard that after my retirement my supervisor was saying that she pushed me out. She failed to understand that I retired a week or two before she was informed and that was how I planned it. I went through the proper channel as instructed and all necessary parties were properly and promptly informed. Well, that is why I left without giving *her* notice. But let us look at this statement. Who says things like that and still expects people to respect him/her? But again, let's look at this statement, 1) whatever document she prepared (Administrative Notice) she was never able to utter one word to me and whatever she wanted to say to me she had to swallow it because she never had a chance to utter or spew her poisonous words to me. Let's be clear, she was doing all sorts of things like training my deputy on certain contracts, without ever discussing it with me and they would meet as soon as I would come into the office. She assigned new procurements to my group knowing full well that we were overloaded and tactics like that. The writing was on the wall that she was up to something when I received an email from her on a Friday afternoon scheduling to meet with me and a human resource person along with an attachment titled "Administrative Notice." I thought about it that night which was the intent I'm sure and it occurred to me to leave this madness because I could. That part.

One of the jokes here is that one of my supervisor's greatest fears was to give my predecessor the title that she denied me but the DC forced her to do when replacing me. It had to be all about her and one of her commonly used phrases were, "it a disaster." Her management style was problem focused.

However, during my short retirement status, I discovered multiple ways of generating revenue, I started taking French lessons and wrote this book. So, who really won here? What she meant for evil, God used it for my good. And my assistant who was helping my supervisor to sabotage my work and hoping to get my job but did not get my job after I left. Where my assistant had a self-serving agenda and allowed herself to be used by my supervisor to vilify me-it did not work. No—not this time devil- not this time.

I strongly sensed that my supervisor wanted to pay me back for corrective actions that I took within my unit, although it was under her direction and support. Such as, writing people up, re-engineering my unit, hiring people, sending people back to their former agency if they did not pass probation, giving raises and promotions and good evaluations. I believe she was jealous of me because she would often say to me that I have a good handle on my unit. However, she would often comment on what was going on in my unit, complaining about the administrative support functions and implying that the administrative staff could never do anything right. It was always something. I realized that she fed off of the energy of drama.

She was not nice to me or anyone else in my position and her modus operandi was to destroy anyone in that position and the DC allowed it. I was NOT going to allow her to destroy me, therefore *she* did not deserve notice regarding my retirement, therefore in my mind she got what she sowed. This is not something that I would encourage others to do, however, there comes a time when one must take a stand and stand firm. You have to pick and choose your battles; this was one battle that I wanted and needed God to fight so I left her in the hands of the Lord.

I chose to believe that God would take care of me so I left my security blanket which was a 9:00-5:00 job; to walk by faith and not by sight. I had had enough of the abusive supervisors and tolerating their issues while in hindsight becoming aware of my issues and dealing with them. Although my retirement has been a period of real self-reflection it has also been an opportunity to move life forward as previously mentioned. Therefore, I had to learn to stop looking back at what I had and try to recapture it but I had to rest in the period of where I am, embrace it and really be okay with it. I moved out of the safe zone into the faith zone. God has not failed me.

After a while, I stopped looking back as I really began to see how God has been taking care of me and enabling me to walk in love and in wisdom. Retirement has become my new norm, not an end but a beginning. By the Grace of God, He helped me to really be okay with my new beginning. I'm settled, happy and have need for nothing.

During this time, I realized a lot about myself, my mistakes, my work ethics and behaviors, I realized where I have been part of the problem in my life as well.

By the Grace of God, I chose to walk away from a toxic environment because the hostility was too expensive for my peace. To work with someone who was angry, hurt and desired to inflict pain on me or anyone in her path-no, I'm good. I was no longer going to subject myself to be an object of her hurt.

I realized that during this time away from the workforce, I spent way too much money for cable, dining out and shopping at high-priced grocery stores. I now have FireStick, eat at home *more often* and shop at Traders Joe's where I would get much more grocery items with $100 then the high-priced grocery store.

I believe that I will re-enter the workforce but as a far better person.

Some of the many lessons that I learned while working with the city are:

- Have a plan B & C.
- If things are not going well for you at your current job, find another one.
- Keep your mouth shut (most of the other oversight agencies who are supposed to correct or remedy problems don't work—I tried, trust me).

- Check yourself, confront yourself and check yourself again.
- Become a "great" decision maker.
- Listen To Jehovah God. Listen. Become A Skillful Listener.
- I was the truth that she (my supervisor) chose to omit—paraphrase from the Black Panther Movie.

Remember this my people, when you point one finger at someone else, there are three fingers pointing back at you.

The common thread that I recognized was that these people/managers chased my problems to avoid their own problems.

When I think of someone in authority who states that there is no institutional racism-I laugh and think what a fool.

WHAT SHOULD HAVE HAPPENED?

I should have gone to another agency.

So here are a few lessons that I learned throughout this experience.

How to Reduce the Misuse of Power in a Workplace

In any successful business, there will be certain people who have more power than others. If wielded appropriately, power can influence others in a positive way. If misused, power manifests as dictatorial and bullying behavior. In a business environment, the chain of command typically includes subordinates who report to supervisors or managers. As a small business owner, employees in leadership roles likely report to you. By promoting a fair and productive work environment, you can reduce the misuse of power in your small business.

Code of Conduct

The misuse of power can disrupt the work environment and inflict mental, physical and/or emotional distress on the victim or victims. Examples of misuse of power include public humiliation, physical attacks, frequently undermining another's effort, disrespectful language, discriminatory comments, yelling, or name calling, excluding or ignoring fellow employees, spreading insidious and untrue rumors, withholding or purposely giving wrong information, and intimidation. The misuse of power is also used to promote self-interests rather than what's best for the team. In your policy manual, define acceptable and unacceptable behaviors. Be specific about the type of behaviors that stem from the misuse of power. State that it is forbidden and that the consequences include termination and enforce it.

Intervention Levels

If you see misuse of power or bullying, address the problem immediately. For an isolated case, have an informal intervention with the alleged bully. Explain that you expect all workers to behave in a professional manner. If someone develops a pattern of misusing their authority, have another meeting showing all data compiled against them, including staff complaints. They might adjust their behavior to reduce the number of complaints. If their behavior persists, implement a more authoritative intervention. If they have exhibited good leadership qualities in the past, there might be an underlying reason for their behavior, such as work stress or personal problems. Establish an evaluation plan with a timeline for them to improve. Explain the importance of accepting responsibility, then explain the outcome if they fail to meet the plan objectives.

Disciplinary Measures

In some cases, you might have to bypass the intervention level. Immediate termination might be necessary if the misuse of power included physical abuse against another employee, or if the person in the position of power uses her authority to do something illegal, such as embezzlement or theft. The level of discipline depends on the impact the abuse of power has on the victim and/or the company. Regardless of the disciplinary measure taken, your policy should include consequences such as verbal and written warnings, suspension, termination, and even legal prosecution.

Leadership Training

A true leader motivates and inspires his employees by leading by example. When subordinates consistently fail to perform satisfactorily, it sometimes reflects poorly on the leader. This puts the leader in a precarious and stressful position. Offer leadership training to your supervisors and managers to help them develop the skills necessary to become a leader who treats his subordinates with fairness and respect.

Support System

The misuse of power can hurt employee morale, lower productivity, cause high employee turnover and frequent absenteeism, cause stress-related illnesses, and harm the company's reputation. These situations often happen when victims feel they have no one to turn to. Create a strong support system for your employees so they don't feel isolated.

Have employee's complete anonymous surveys to gauge whether power is being misused in the company. In your policy manual, outline the steps employees can take to file a complaint. Assure staff that investigations into misuse of power will be handled promptly, fairly, and confidentially. Listen impartially to the alleged perpetrator and victim and obtain as much proof as possible before arriving at a conclusion. If necessary, hire a workplace consultant to act as a mediator in employee disputes and to help you draft policies and procedures that address the misuse of power.

Where Do You Draw the Line?

In many such instances, it's possible for a supervisor to engage in behavior that's unpleasant or troubling but behavior that doesn't automatically rise to a level that a court of law would find legally abusive. For example, a generally gruff supervisor might treat one employee gently. A supervisor might tell a subordinate to get him coffee. Without being more specific, a male supervisor might tell a female subordinate that she "looks great." With an approaching deadline, a supervisor might ask a subordinate to get her a sandwich from the commissary on the grounds that she hasn't eaten all day and that she can't take time to get it herself.

To better understand if you're stuck with an inconsiderate boss or that you have cause to report the behavior to Human Resources, a state labor commission, or the Equal Opportunity Commission —first consider if the action is occasional or is ongoing. Then, consider the effect of the behavior on the company in general terms; consider the effect on the supervisor's subordinates; and consider the effect on you. Is it a bit rude or is it troubling? Does it affect how well this supervisor's department functions? A boss who asks you to get him coffee may not be your favorite supervisor, but if it happens only occasionally, there are probably better ways to deal with the problem other than filing a report.

One way of dealing with a lot of bad behavior that's not bad enough to be reportable is to turn the tables. This is a response recommended by Gary Namie, the director of the Workplace Bullying Institute. "Fetching coffee isn't in my job description, but, hey, I'll do it for you this time if you'll do it for me next time." "You know, I could have gone all day without hearing that. Nice try...."

But if the behavior is objectionable enough—and particularly if it's recurrent—you may have to take further action. Bad behavior that doesn't have consequences will probably lead to worse behavior, in the future.

Who Do You Report to and What Do You Report?

The first thing you should do when you realize the abuse is serious is to keep a written record of every instance. Whenever possible, keep track of witnesses.

What you do next depends on your workplace. Often, companies have written codes of conduct in place that include who you should report to and how you should do it. In the absence of a special unit that deals with this kind of problem, contact Human Resources.

Write down your thoughts and questions about this chapter. Write it down and make it plain (Habakkuk 2:2-3)

_____
_____
_____
_____
_____
_____
_____

Consider these questions.

1) Would you agree that a lack of "self" helps immunize you against hurts?

2) Are angry people self-centered?

_____
_____
_____
_____
_____
_____
_____

CHAPTER 6
SIDE BAR

Let's talk, Real talk

HAVE YOU EVER BEEN?

<u>Harassed</u> - Harassment is defined as words or behavior that threatens, intimidates or demeans a person. Harassment is unwanted, uninvited and unwelcome and causes nuisance, alarm, or substantial emotional distress without any legitimate purpose.

<u>Stalked</u> - Stalking is defined as the act or crime of willfully and repeatedly following or harassing another person in circumstances that would cause a reasonable person to fear injury or death especially because of express or implied threats.

<u>Misunderstood</u> - Misunderstood is defined as incorrectly interpreted or understood.

Write down your thoughts and make it plain (Habakkuk 2:2-3)

CHAPTER 7
KEEP IT GOING AND KEEP IT MOVING

"I have failed far more times than I have succeeded. You will never succeed. You will never succeed more than you fail. When you fail, it's a part of the process. Keep going. Who you know that gets it right all the time? That's impossible. Every time you fail, you're one step closer to your goal." Steve Harvey.

By the Grace of Almighty God, He helped me to turn my pain into power by teaching me that if people work together for long periods of time-even if they are fighting with each other—be quiet. Just quietly observe and keep it moving. Because there is always something that connects them and keeps them together and they will use that "connection" against you, if needed. Keep it going and keep it moving.

Bishop TD Jakes said it best, "people who don't even like each other will get together to hate you."

When you move from one city agency to another, people tend to know someone in the agency that you are going to, and the new agency people develop a predetermined idea of you. They either slander you or support you. If you are being slandered, you don't have a chance to prove yourself because the gossip begins and continues to follow you until you leave or retire. It could be a vicious cycle of unending gossip about you. Never leaving you room to breathe. It's called character assassination. Keep it going and keep it moving.

I may not have been physically murdered by aggressive and racist people; however, my character was assassinated (murdered) by someone who saw me as a threat, became suspicious of me and shared those thoughts and attitudes with others. Keep it going and keep it moving.

The staff member who worked with my former supervisor to sabotage my work was hoping to be promoted to my job but was disappointed because she did not get my job. My understanding is that she abruptly took a medical leave of absence, thus leaving my replacement without any administrative support which was vital to both units.

I believe God gave me a way of escape (which I did not take) to go to another agency before I retired but that agency had people jumping ship. They always had positions available and whenever we had a position available there were always multiple resumes from this agency. Whenever we chose to interview people from this particular agency it was not good. We always got a sense that something was dreadfully wrong. So, I had to keep it going and keep it moving.

Should I ever return to work, I would not go back looking for inefficiencies and deficiencies within an office but rather identify those policies and procedures that work and support and build upon those foundations.

During my short-term retirement I learned to look at myself because I was the common denominator. That is not to say that all I experienced was not at the hands of, initiation of, hatred of and jealousy of others. That is not to say that I was not targeted.

What I am saying is that I have chosen to look at myself as well because I was the common denominator.

Here are some post-retirement observations:

My former supervisor did not get a chance to put anything in my personnel file.

My former supervisor did not get a chance to drag me through the mud like she was hoping to do.

My former supervisor did not get a chance to spew her poisonous words at me.

My former supervisor had to keep all that venom in her all bottled up and knowing her, that ate her up. Because she never got to fulfill her plan against me.

I became aware of how to redirect my funds and invest—especially in black-owned businesses.

I wrote this book.

I self-reflected and identified the error of my ways, sat with the effects of them, took responsibility and grew.

Started taking French classes.

Becoming a better (active) listener.

Becoming a better decision maker.

I was able to identify a great deal of wasteful spending. Thus, I became a better steward of my resources.

I learned how to cook-again.

My former supervisor wasn't able to contact my employer (new agency) and spew her poison.

So, who really won?

Why is self-reflection so important? "It's possible to not know who you really are." TD Jakes.

"Self-reflection or self-confrontation must become a part of your everyday life if you are to avoid the hypocrisy of judging the failures of others without first examining your own life." John C. Broger.

A former City employee said, "it feels so good to work in an environment where my supervisor isn't waiting to sabotage my work or waiting for me to fail to try to prove that I'm not as good as other people say."

My (earthly) Father

In fact, some years ago when I was visiting with my father when he was hospitalized, I paid for his telephone and television bills, shopped for undergarments and pajamas because he did not have anything. When he was released days later and was in a hurry to get home to his new girlfriend. When I dropped him off at this house I could smell a strange stench in his house. I could smell it. Just to be clear, I just associated that "stench" on him and in his apartment to witchcraft. I don't know what witchcraft smells like-again it's just what I associated my father with-as did his siblings-my aunts and uncles. After that I did not hear from my father again, he stopped calling and did not return my calls which was his usual behavior. So I had to keep it going and keep it moving.

The fact that my father left my mother with three children for another woman with three children was the root of my anger with my father. We hardly heard from him and whenever my mother called him for money to buy food he never showed up.

I was so caught up in my anger that although my father tried reaching out to me for at least a year before he passed, I would not respond. I stayed in my anger because of what I believed about him for so many years, which was the practice of witchcraft. He and his then girlfriend were deep in witchcraft and the entire family was aware of it which I believe they used to take my mother's life at such an early age. I didn't know what I know now-spiritually-so I couldn't fight for my mother.

When my father passed away, I did not physically attend his funeral, it was during COVID, and it was filmed although a seat was reserved for me, I didn't go; I interfered and messed up with the writing of the obituary that my cousin was kind enough to write. I didn't take the time to say goodbye to my father but now I am turning my pain into power, by way of saying goodbye to my father now-*goodbye daddy.*

The moral of the story is that when you fail even in relationships, keep it going and keep it moving.

Let's be clear that keep it going and keep it moving doesn't mean you adopt a callous attitude. You should learn from it, acknowledge your failure(s) and humble yourself then you keep it going and keep it moving.

Write down your thoughts and questions about this chapter. Write it down and make it plain (Habakkuk 2:2-3)

_____

_____

_____

_____

_____

CHAPTER 8
POWER POINTS

Power points are power-filled thought provoking quotes that could be incorporated in our thought process.

You may encounter defeats, but you must not be defeated. (Maya Angelou)

I never lose, I either win or learn. (Nelson Mandela)

Always stay gracious, the best revenge is your paper. (Beyonce Knowles-Carter)

They can't kill the truth, so they assassinate your character. (Australian Independent Media)

They couldn't break your spirit, so they will try to assassinate your character. (@inspirepositivelife)

You don't know the heart of a person until they have your secrets. (RC Blakes)

I AM ENOUGH!! I DON'T CARE!! I ALWAYS WIN!! (RC Blakes)

Spineless for love and spineless for attention; But I know better now. (author unknown)

Truth is confrontational. (A personal friend)

No one has to fail in order for me to succeed. (Pastor Creflo Dollar)

Make a decision not to be entangled in the affairs of the world.

Make your mind up to be happy. Set your will to be happy and to line up with the Word of God. (Pastor Creflo Dollar)

Whatever you don't deal with, it will come back around and deal with you. (unknown)

Some people live to collect enemies and throw away friends. (unknown)

The more you run away from your sins the more exhausted you are when they catch up to you. (unknown)

Come out of every situation with a lesson. (unknown)

Judge yourself, don't be so quick to put things off onto other people. (unknown)

Sometimes things are much stronger in my head. (unknown)

They chased my problems to avoid their own problems. (All Rise)

Instead of exalting yourself, examine yourself. (unknown)

Measure twice, cut once. (former colleague)

A lie gets around the world before the truth has a chance to put its pants on. (unknown)

Be afraid to believe a lie. (Mike Murdock)

It's not about how you fall but about how you get up. (unknown)

When you're through changing....you're through. (unknown)

There's nothing as powerful as a changed mind. (Bishop TD Jakes)

Don't set yourself on fire to keep others warm. (author unknown)

The mouth that eats cannot talk. (African Proverb)

No matter how long, the day is sure to come. (African Proverb)

If you verify it may cost you, but if you don't verify it may cost you everything. (Reesa Teesa)

CHAPTER 9
I NOW REALIZE

I *now* realize that my mother and brother went through some dark and difficult times between 1990-1991. Apparently, my mother was injured on the job and applied for worker's compensation and as most of us are aware it's not an easy task dealing with this agency. Needless-to-say, they denied my mother of her benefits and she was forced to appeal that decision which took a significant amount of time for a favorable decision to be made on her behalf. Therefore, my mother and brother struggled financially to make ends meet. Although my mother and I spoke often, I didn't know exactly what was going on.

After some time, worker's compensation came through and she was granted benefits, retroactively. Upon such, my mother and brother decided to relocate to Florida where my sister and her family moved some years earlier. We had not seen my sister since she moved, so I traveled with them to Florida, as they moved in August which is my birthday month.

During that time, I was a part of an intercessory ministry at my church and one of the many things we prayed about was for the salvation of our loved ones. One Friday night, one of the pastor's felt impressed for us to cry out to God for our loved ones. The prayer atmosphere became intense. I recall praying earnestly for my family and that Sunday morning while I was at home praying, I felt a sense of urgency from the Holy Spirit telling me to call my mother which I did but she couldn't talk because of some breathing issues. A day or two later my brother called me crying hysterically that my mother had passed away.

She moved to Florida in August, 1991 and died in September, 1991. Needless to say, we were all stunned and my brother took it particularly hard because he believes, to this day, that my mother left him after going through whatever difficulties they faced together while awaiting her worker's compensation approval. I still believe that my mother went to say goodbye to my sister in Florida-unbeknownst to my mother.

I later learned that my mother suffered from a number of health issues such as high blood pressure and heart disease. Undoubtedly, preparing for my mother's funeral was one of the most difficult things that I ever encountered and what made it more difficult is that I had to do *everything* while dealing with all my emotions. I was in a daze most of the time and it was one big blur (ugh face emoji).

I think my mom felt abandoned by me and perhaps misunderstood my involvement with the intercessory ministry, where we prayed all night Mondays through Sundays. Believe me although it may have been frowned upon by people who did not understand but let me tell you it was my spiritual saving grace-even to this day. We were all well-balanced professionals but were committed to our intercessory calling which was prayer seven days a week according to the prayer schedule.

For clarity, the members of this ministry were required to attend Friday night bible study and attend one prayer meeting during Sunday service. We were given prayer requests from around the country which we prayed over for a period of time. There were captains and co-captains assigned to a particular prayer shift which was morning, afternoon and evening.

Believe me that was one of the best years of my life and the original members who were a part of the development of this ministry, we're all great friends to this day.

I *now* realize, in hindsight, how wrong I've been on so many occasions which is quite painful because my mother was trying to talk to me but I couldn't hear her because I was caught up in my own world. Nonetheless, there is an ache in my heart because I think that I failed my mother, again, unbeknownst to me at that time.

I *now* realize that I should have stopped to listen to her more, visited her more and talked to her more.

I *now* realize that I owe my mother an apology. Mommy, I apologize to you from the bottom of my heart for not hearing you and for not being there for you the way that I should have been there for you.

I *now* realize that I owe my brother an apology and a debt I will certainly pay. I apologize to you Lee for not being there for you and mommy when you needed me the most.

I *now* realize that I need to *watch myself* and pray and pray again and pray again some more, thus checking my motives in everything I do (pause and calmly think about that).

I *now* realize that I didn't know that I was me.

Write down your thoughts and questions about this chapter. Write it down and make it plain (Habakkuk 2:2-3)

_____

_____

_____

_____

_____

_____

Special thanks to my late mother whom I hope would be proud of me and my wonderful daughter for her loving support.

Please note that your purchase will allow donations to be made to empower, elevate and protect individuals to live their best authentic lives for peace and happiness.

CHAPTER 10
KEYS

A key can be defined as an instrument to provide solutions, to gain entrance and possession of new possibilities. Think about using the following keys to practice and meditate on each month. Also, consider challenging yourself to conduct a monthly study of each key that may help you to realize that you didn't know that you were you.

January - Love
February - Joy
March - Peace
April - Patience
May - Kindness
June - Goodness
July - Self Control
August - Success
September - Health
October - Prosperity
November - Honesty
December - Self Confrontation/Self Reflection

LOVE

According to the Webster Dictionary, love is a strong affection for another arising out of kinship or personal ties.

Write down your thoughts and experience for the month of January.

JOY

According to the Webster Dictionary, joy is a feeling of great pleasure or happiness that comes from success, good fortune, or a sense of well-being.

Write down your thoughts and experience for the month of February.

PEACE

According to the Webster Dictionary, peace is a state of tranquility or quiet; freedom from upsetting thoughts or feelings.

Write down your thoughts and experience for the month of March.

_____
_____
_____
_____
_____
_____
_____
_____
_____
_____
_____
_____
_____
_____
_____

PATIENCE

According to the Webster Dictionary, patience is steadfast despite opposition, difficulty or adversity.

Write down your thoughts and experience for the month of April.

_____

_____

_____

_____

_____

_____

_____

_____

_____

_____

_____

_____

_____

KINDNESS

According to the Webster Dictionary, kindness is a sympathetic or helpful nature.

Write down your thoughts and experience for the month of May.

_____
_____
_____
_____
_____
_____
_____
_____
_____
_____
_____
_____
_____
_____
_____

GOODNESS

According to the Webster Dictionary, goodness is the quality or state of being good; morally excellent; virtuous; righteous; pious.

Write down your thoughts and experience for the month of June.

_____
_____
_____
_____
_____
_____
_____
_____
_____
_____
_____
_____
_____
_____

SELF-CONTROL

According to the Webster Dictionary, self-control is restraint exercised over one's own impulses, emotions or desires.

Write down your thoughts and experience for the month of July.

_____
_____
_____
_____
_____
_____
_____
_____
_____
_____
_____
_____
_____
_____

SUCCESS

According to the Webster Dictionary, success is a degree or measure of succeeding; favorable or desired outcome; the attainment of wealth, favor or eminence.

Write down your thoughts and experience for the month of August.

_____
_____
_____
_____
_____
_____
_____
_____
_____
_____
_____
_____
_____
_____

HEALTH

According to the Webster Dictionary, health is a state of being free from illness or injury; the condition of being sound in body, mind, or spirit.

Write down your thoughts and experience for the month of September.

PROSPERITY

According to the Webster Dictionary, prosperity is the state of being prosperous or successful.

Write down your thoughts and experience for the month of October.

_____

_____

_____

_____

_____

_____

_____

_____

_____

_____

_____

_____

HONESTY

According to the Webster Dictionary, honesty is adherence to the facts; sincerity; fairness and straightforwardness of conduct.

Write down your thoughts and experience for the month of November.

SELF CONFRONTATION/SELF REFLECTION

According to the Webster Dictionary, self-confrontation is defined as self-analysis; the examination of one's attitudes, behaviors and shortcomings to provide an impetus to change and to gain insight into how one is perceived by others.

According to the Webster Dictionary, self-reflection is defined as taking the time to think about, meditate on, evaluate and give serious thought to your behaviors, thoughts, attitudes, motivations and desires.

Write down your thoughts and experience for the month of December.

_____
_____
_____
_____
_____
_____
_____
_____
_____
_____
_____
_____
_____
_____
_____

CHAPTER II
THE CONCLUSION

Please remember that I'm sharing my story, my thoughts, my opinions, my experiences and keys because……….

I didn't know I was me (Bishop TD Jakes)

www.ingramcontent.com/pod-product-compliance
Lightning Source LLC
Chambersburg PA
CBHW050224100526
44585CB00017BA/1950